Treehouses
&
Playhouses
YOU CAN BUILD

✳ Other Books by David and Jeanie Stiles

Workshops You Can Build
Treehouses, Huts & Forts
Treehouses You Can Actually Build
Fun Projects For You and the Kids
Cabins:
  A Guide to Building Your Own Retreat
Sheds—A Do-it-Yourself Guide
Playhouses You Can Build
Rustic Retreats
Garden Retreats

Treehouses & Playhouses

YOU CAN BUILD

David & Jeanie Stiles

Designs and Illustrations
by
David Stiles

Gibbs Smith, Publisher
Salt Lake City

First Edition

10 09 08 07 06   5 4 3 2 1

Published by
Gibbs Smith, Publisher
P.O. Box 667
Layton, Utah 84041

Orders: 1.800.835.4993
www.gibbs-smith.com

Designed by Kurt Wahlner
Printed and bound in Canada

Library of Congress Cataloging-in-Publication Data

Stiles, David R.
  Treehouses and playhouses you can build / David and
Jeanie Stiles.—1st ed.
  p. cm.
  ISBN 1-58685-780-0
  1. Tree houses. 2. Children's playhouses. I. Title: Tree houses
and playhouses you can build. II. Stiles, Jeanie. Title.

TH4885.S755 2006
690'.89—dc22

2006007989

To lofty trees and those who dwell in them.

Secrets

In all of our hearts there is a place for secrets,
A place to go—ours alone, not for sharing—
To remember wonderful joys and sad regrets
And the countless times of wondrous caring.

In our childhood 'twas a stairway or closet dark,
Where we could huddle with ourselves and dream,
Or a chair remote, or a corner window over the park
Where we could see, unseen, developing our life scheme.

And now we see that child in our children, girls and boys,
And their children, too, with their secret places,
Matching our sad moments mixed with joys,
An unending heritage marking their hearts and faces.

—C. Edwin Fitzgerald

To Our Readers

Since many of our readers invariably change our plans to fit their particular needs, we assume that they will seek qualified, licensed architects or engineers to make more detailed plans for submission to their local building and health departments, as required.

NOTE: Every effort has been made to design all the projects in this book to be safe and easy to build; however, it is impossible to predict every situation and the ability of each carpenter who builds our projects. Therefore, it is advised that the reader seek advice from a competent, on-site expert.

Disclaimer: *David and Jeanie Stiles make no express or implied warranties, including warranties of performance, merchantability and fitness for a particular purpose, regarding this information. Your use of this information is at your own risk. You assume full responsibility and risk of loss resulting from the use of this information. The authors and publisher will not be responsible for any direct, special, indirect, incidental, consequential or punitive damages or any other damages whatsoever.*

Please visit our Web site at
www.stilesdesigns.com
and send us photographs of your
treehouses and playhouses.

Stiles
Designs

STILESDESIGNS

CONTENTS

Acknowledgments

We would like to thank Suzanne Taylor and Christopher Robbins for their enthusiasm and for sharing the same vision that we have for this book. Many thanks also to our editor, Kristi G. Valdez, for her professionalism and hard work, which helped bring this book to fruition. In addition, we are most indebted to Simon Jutras for his invaluable photographic skills and gifted vision.

We are also grateful to all the treehouse and playhouse builders who have written to us and sent us photos of their terrific projects—each one a unique structure. Many have courageously taken our advice, gone out on a limb and built their own treehouses. If only space had allowed, we would have included all our readers' projects in the book, as each one is a work of art!

ABOUT THIS BOOK

Although *Treehouses and Playhouses You Can Build* does include beautiful photos, it is not a coffee-table book. It is a hands-on, do-it-yourself book that you can take to your building site and refer to as you are working. Since construction directions can often be confusing, we have tried to make ours as clear as possible, for both adults and children, by using drawings and step-by-step instructions. For the majority of the projects, we have included dimensional plans with clear, easy-to-follow illustrations and a materials list. Exact dimensions are impossible for some projects. No two trees are the same shape or size; however, we have included practical solutions and construction tips that can be applied to all of the play structures. We have also included two photography sections that will provide you with inspiration and ideas.

Some projects take an afternoon to build, others may take a summer. Some require only a handsaw and a screwdriver, while others may require more sophisticated power tools. We don't expect you to have extensive knowledge in woodworking or to have expensive tools at your disposal. We have avoided using unfamiliar, technical words, but when they are necessary, we have followed them with clarification in parenthesis.

Needless to say, some of the projects in this book are beyond the skills of the average youngster and will require the help of an adult. Children should not operate power tools until they are in their mid-teens and, even then, they should be closely supervised and taught how to use the tools safely. In the meantime, children should be given a way to participate in the process by helping with design decisions and working with simple hand tools like saws, screwdrivers, hammers, and sanding blocks. Family meetings are an important part of designing your treehouse or playhouse. Everyone should have a "wish list" and be allowed to contribute to the design and use of the project.

We have designed all the projects in the book to use the least amount of expensive materials. We encourage our readers you to use or substitute materials you might find around the house, not only to save money, but also to recycle materials and reduce the amount of waste. When cutting out pieces from a 4 x 8 sheet of plywood, we have done our best to use the entire piece, and show this clearly in our cutting plans. We advise against buying endangered wood or working with wood that contains dangerous chemicals.

Most readers rarely follow our plans exactly. Often, our readers are most proud of the changes they make to the original design, enabling them to create a project unique to their family. Our wish is for you to take our design ideas and adapt them to your specific situation, whether it be in a tree, a backyard, or on four posts in the ground. Be inventive!

BASIC BUILDING INFORMATION

Tools

We have tried to illustrate the most basic, essential tools required for building the majority of the treehouses and playhouses in this book. See illustrations on pages 13–15.

For projects with more difficult construction directions (such as the Pie-Rat Ship Playhouse and the Victorian Playhouse), we have suggested a few power tools. For building up in a tree, battery-operated tools are helpful.

Hand Tools

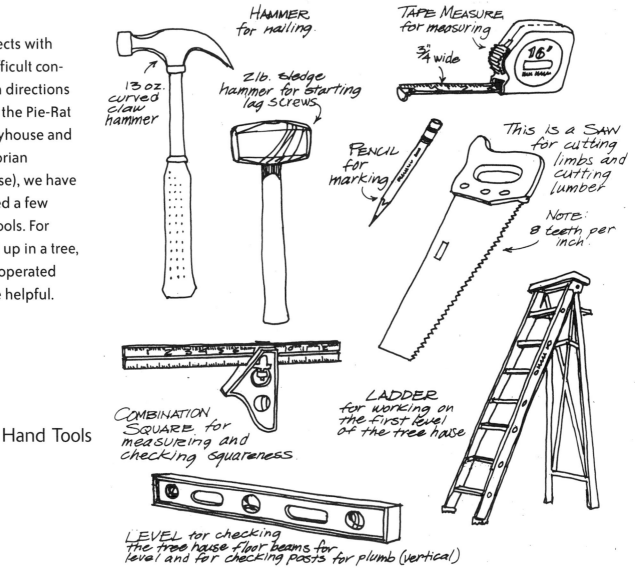

HAMMER for nailing.

13 oz. curved claw hammer

2 lb. sledge hammer for starting lag screws

PENCIL for marking.

TAPE MEASURE for measuring

¾" wide

16'

This is a SAW for cutting limbs and cutting lumber

NOTE: 8 teeth per inch.

COMBINATION SQUARE for measuring and checking squareness.

LADDER for working on the first level of the tree house

LEVEL for checking the tree house floor beams for level and for checking posts for plumb (vertical)

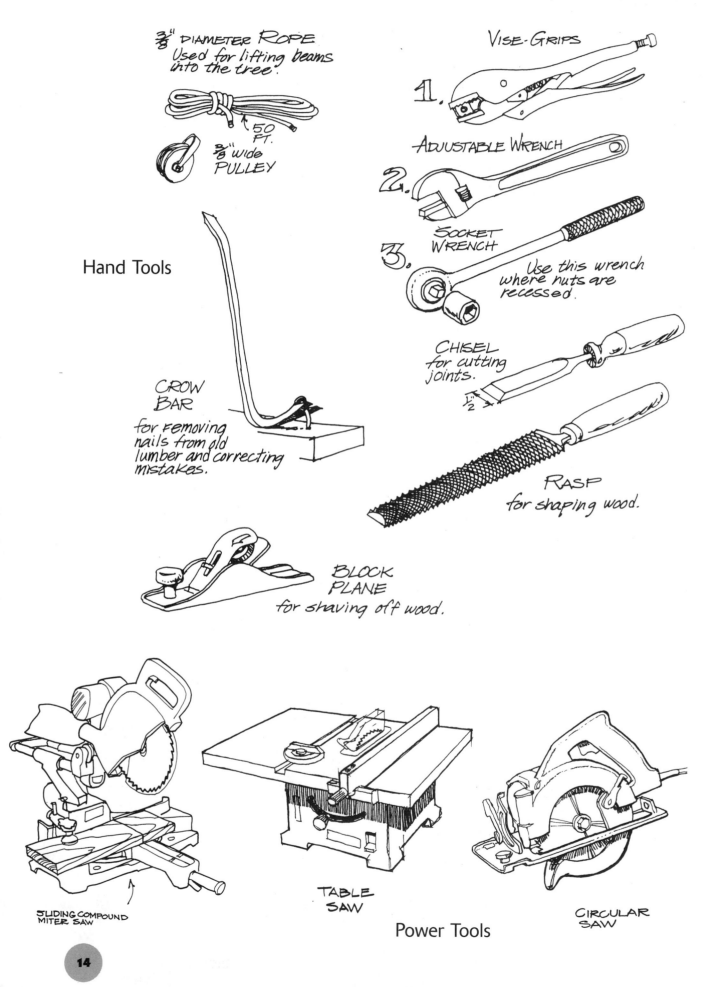

Choose one of Three Types of Wrenches.

$\frac{3}{8}$" diameter Rope
Used for lifting beams into the tree.

50 FT.

$\frac{3}{8}$" wide PULLEY

Vise-Grips

1.

Adjustable Wrench

2.

Socket Wrench

3.

Use this wrench where nuts are recessed.

Hand Tools

CROW BAR
for removing nails from old lumber and correcting mistakes.

Chisel
for cutting joints.

$\frac{1}{2}$"

RASP
for shaping wood.

BLOCK PLANE
for shaving off wood.

SLIDING COMPOUND MITER SAW

TABLE SAW

CIRCULAR SAW

Power Tools

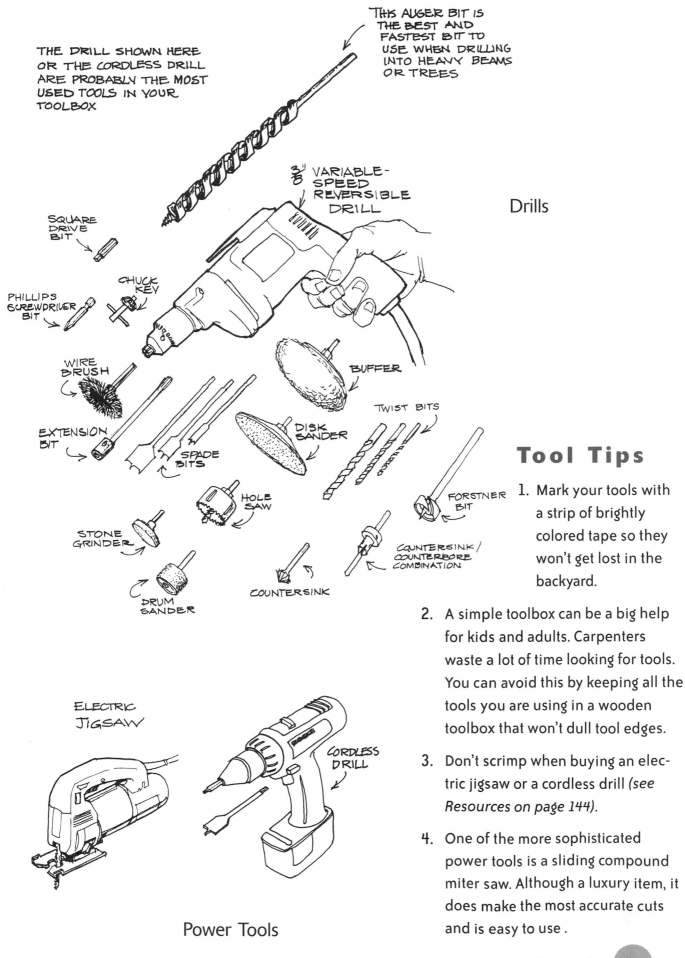

THIS AUGER BIT IS THE BEST AND FASTEST BIT TO USE WHEN DRILLING INTO HEAVY BEAMS OR TREES

THE DRILL SHOWN HERE OR THE CORDLESS DRILL ARE PROBABLY THE MOST USED TOOLS IN YOUR TOOLBOX

3/8" VARIABLE-SPEED REVERSIBLE DRILL

Drills

SQUARE DRIVE BIT

CHUCK KEY

PHILLIPS SCREWDRIVER BIT

BUFFER

WIRE BRUSH

TWIST BITS

EXTENSION BIT

DISK SANDER

SPADE BITS

FORSTNER BIT

HOLE SAW

STONE GRINDER

COUNTERSINK / COUNTERBORE COMBINATION

COUNTERSINK

DRUM SANDER

ELECTRIC JIGSAW

CORDLESS DRILL

Power Tools

Tool Tips

1. Mark your tools with a strip of brightly colored tape so they won't get lost in the backyard.

2. A simple toolbox can be a big help for kids and adults. Carpenters waste a lot of time looking for tools. You can avoid this by keeping all the tools you are using in a wooden toolbox that won't dull tool edges.

3. Don't scrimp when buying an electric jigsaw or a cordless drill *(see Resources on page 144).*

4. One of the more sophisticated power tools is a sliding compound miter saw. Although a luxury item, it does make the most accurate cuts and is easy to use .

Lumber and Materials

Before buying lumber, take inventory of any leftover lumber you might have lying around the house and see if it can be incorporated in the design. Second-hand lumber can often be found at the town dump or at construction sites where new houses are being built. Speak to the general contractor and ask him to show you his pile of discarded wood. In most cases, you will be doing him a favor if you remove the leftover lumber, as he will have to pay carting and dump fees to get rid of it. Make sure, however, to get his approval before taking it.

Once you have a materials list with the types and lengths of lumber you will need, you can order it by phone and have the lumber company deliver the wood, at no charge, to your house. The drawback is if you are an infrequent customer, they may not go to the trouble of picking out straight pieces, leaving you with the warped ones. One way around this is to order 10 percent more lumber than you need and have them take back the bad pieces. To do this, however, they may charge you 15 percent storage and handling fee.

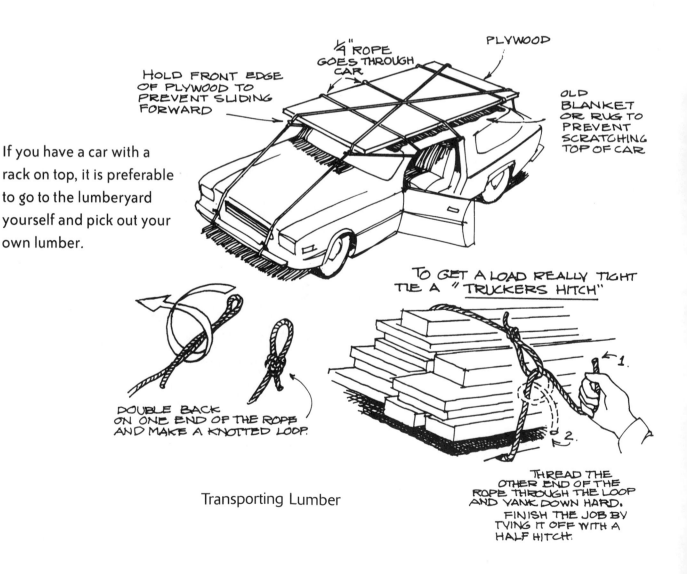

HOLD FRONT EDGE OF PLYWOOD TO PREVENT SLIDING FORWARD

¼" ROPE GOES THROUGH CAR

PLYWOOD

OLD BLANKET OR RUG TO PREVENT SCRATCHING TOP OF CAR

If you have a car with a rack on top, it is preferable to go to the lumberyard yourself and pick out your own lumber.

DOUBLE BACK ON ONE END OF THE ROPE AND MAKE A KNOTTED LOOP.

TO GET A LOAD REALLY TIGHT TIE A "TRUCKERS HITCH"

THREAD THE OTHER END OF THE ROPE THROUGH THE LOOP AND YANK DOWN HARD. FINISH THE JOB BY TYING IT OFF WITH A HALF HITCH.

Transporting Lumber

Lumber Tips

1. Don't be afraid to ask questions of the "yardmen" who work with the lumber and should be able to answer most of your questions. They are there to help.

2. Bring a tape measure.

3. Don't pretend that you are a professional builder in order to get a discount. They know who is and who isn't.

Sighting Lumber

4. Check the lumber piles before you pay to make sure they have the pieces you want.

5. Clear (knot-free) lumber is three to four times more expensive than #2-grade lumber (with knots); therefore, look for clear sections in #2 boards and cut away the knotted sections. These can be used for non-critical jobs. All #2 boards are construction-grade lumber.

6. Spend time holding each board at arm's length and sight down the edges (two walls) of the board to make sure they are straight.

7. Lumberyards often stack their structural framing lumber outside where it may become water-soaked and heavy. For this reason, try home-improvement centers where the lumber is stored indoors.

HEARTWOOD (HARDER)

GRAIN

SAPWOOD (SOFTER)

CROWN

CHECK

BOWED

CUPPED

TWISTED

KNOTTED

SPLIT

Be on the lookout for:

Lumber Sizes

Standard lumber is sold in lengths of 2-foot increments, starting at 6 feet long. Don't expect the lumberyard to cut a piece shorter than 6 feet, which would leave them with a piece they can't sell. Lumber is sold in "nominal" dimensions. For example, a 2x4 actually measures only $1\frac{1}{2}$ x $3\frac{1}{2}$ inches. This is a result of the final machine surfacing and the shrinkage as it dries. As you can see by the illustration, this discrepancy diminishes to $\frac{1}{4}$ inch when the width of the board goes beyond $5\frac{1}{2}$ inches.

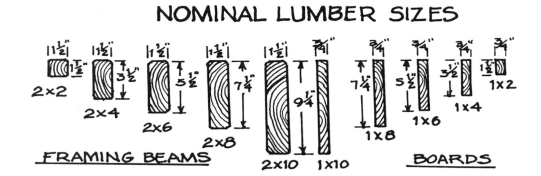

NOMINAL LUMBER SIZES

FRAMING BEAMS   BOARDS

Pressure-Treated Lumber

Whenever wood is in contact with the ground or in a high-moisture area, use pressure-treated lumber for building. Generally, it is not necessary to use it in a treehouse where there is fresh air circulating around the wood. Several years ago the Environmental Protection Agency forced lumber companies to eliminate the arsenic in formula CCA (Chromated Copper Arsenate) in pressure-treated lumber to the safer ACQ (Alkaline Copper Quaternary) type. Even though the EPA now approves ACQ for playground equipment, precautions should still be taken not to breathe in the dust when sanding or sawing through the wood.

Although considerably heavier than its counterpart Douglas fir, pressure-treated wood is stronger and often has a beautiful grain since it is normally made out of southern pine. Once it has dried out (about two months), it can be stained to look like expensive teak. (*See Resources:* Osmose Wood Preserving, Inc.)

Plywood

Plywood comes in thicknesses ranging from $\frac{1}{8}$ to $\frac{3}{4}$ inch and is commonly sold in 4x8-foot sheets. Thicker (1 inch) and longer (10 feet) sheets can be special ordered. Make sure to measure the thickness of a sheet before you begin your project as it can vary between manufacturers.

For the most part, to build treehouses and playhouses you should use "exterior" plywood

> **Tip:**
> Pressure-treated boards may vary in width dramatically because of the treatment process.

made from "plies" of wood joined together with a glue that will stand up to all sorts of weather.

Logs

If you live in an area where there is access to trees, consider using logs instead of costly milled lumber. Look for the seasoned dead logs leaning against other trees or lying on the ground. Check to make sure that they are not rotten by removing the bark with a spoke shave (drawknife).

The Hobbit Treehouse was partially built from cedar logs found lying on the ground of a friend's property. A treehouse built using tree limbs can be very aesthetically pleasing. The limbs, as they weather, appear to become part of the tree itself and give the impression that the limbs of the treehouse and the tree itself grew together of their own accord.

Some counties or towns have designated areas where you can remove dead wood in order to prevent forest fires. For the same reason, some landowners will be happy to have you take their dead trees, but be sure to get their written permission before you begin. Also check with your local tree-removal experts (found in the yellow pages) and ask where they dump their trees. You may be able to strike a deal where they save exactly the right kind of logs for you.

Purchased Logs

If you can't find logs lying on the ground, you can find them at garden supply centers. Cedar poles, used for supporting freshly planted saplings, cost far less than standard lumber and look nicer. Working with logs and poles is more time consuming than working with milled lumber but the results are well worth it.

Joining Logs

Joining logs together is difficult because their cylindrical shape makes a poor bearing surface.

Step 1

To make a good joint between two logs, it is necessary to provide a flat surface on each log where they join. To do this, use a hand saw to make two slanted cuts, one-third of the way through each of the two logs.

Step 2

Use a chisel to remove the wood between the cuts and clean up the notch using a rasp (a course file for shaping tight spaces). If done correctly, the two logs will join together as though they are biting each other.

Step 3

Attach the logs with a screw that can be hidden by a wooden peg if you desire.

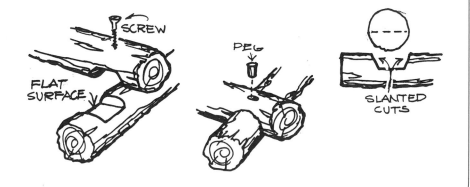

SCREW

FLAT SURFACE

PEG

SLANTED CUTS

Making a Peg 'n Hole Joint

Another way to join logs (or poles if building a railing) is called a "peg 'n hole" joint. Keep in mind that the "peg 'n hole" joint can only be used on one end of the railing, since the ends of the railing are fixed. Shape the other end of the railing to match the outside curve of the post and join it with two screws.

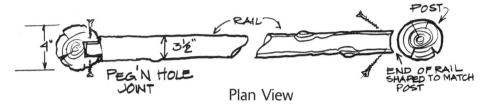

Plan View

Step 1

Drill a $1^1/_2$-inch-diameter hole in the post that will receive the peg or tenon. Use a $1^1/_2$-inch hole saw to make a circular cut in the end of the railing.

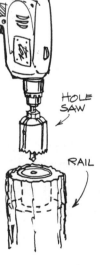

Using a Hole Saw

POST

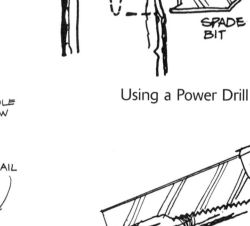

Using a Power Drill

Step 2

If you don't have a hole saw, you can use an ordinary hand saw to make a partial cut around the end of the railing and chisel away the outer layer of the wood.

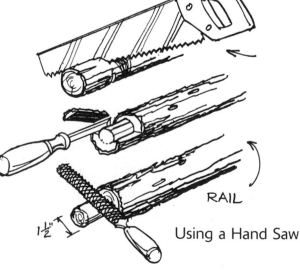

Using a Hand Saw

Step 3

Use a rasp to shape the end of the rail into a 1$\frac{1}{2}$-inch-diameter peg (tenon).

Step 4

Insert the peg end of the rail into the hole of the post for a test fit.

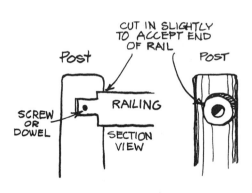

Step 5

To make a perfect fit, chisel a slight depression in the post the same size as the diameter of the rail. To hold the peg in the hole, drill a pilot hole through the side of the post into the peg and insert a small dowel or screw.

Mini-Ties

One alternative to using logs is to use pressure-treated mini-ties, sometimes referred to as landscape logs. Measuring 3x5 inches, they are flat on two sides and come 8-feet long and cost less than $7 each. You can find them at home improvement centers and most lumberyards. They are excellent for structural framing or for posts since they can be placed in contact with the ground without rotting. In a treehouse they look like natural logs and the green color can be stained grey or brown to match the tree. (*See Resources:* Osmose Wood Preserving, Inc.)

These mini-ties are pressure-treated with ACQ, eliminating the arsenic that used to be put in the wood. They are stronger than common white pine and can support a great deal of weight without bending. As with any lumber, it is to your advantage to hand pick the mini-ties and check to make sure they are straight. The nice thing about mini-ties is that they look like round logs but at the same time have two flat sides making it easier to join pieces together.

Bamboo

Although bamboo has been used for many years in Asian countries, it has more recently become a popular building material in the United States. It has many advantages, including its renewable, fast growing qualities, and is lightweight and, if treated correctly, long lasting. Joining pieces of bamboo together can be done in several ways and can result in a spectacular looking treehouse.

Don't use bamboo that you have found growing in the woods, as it needs to be processed to keep it from quickly decaying. Professionals usually do this by soaking it in a boric acid solution and drying it for several days in the sun. There are many suppliers of treated bamboo in the United States *(see Resources)* where it can be purchased at a reasonable price. Since bamboo has become more popular, many garden supply outlets carry it.

Joining Bamboo

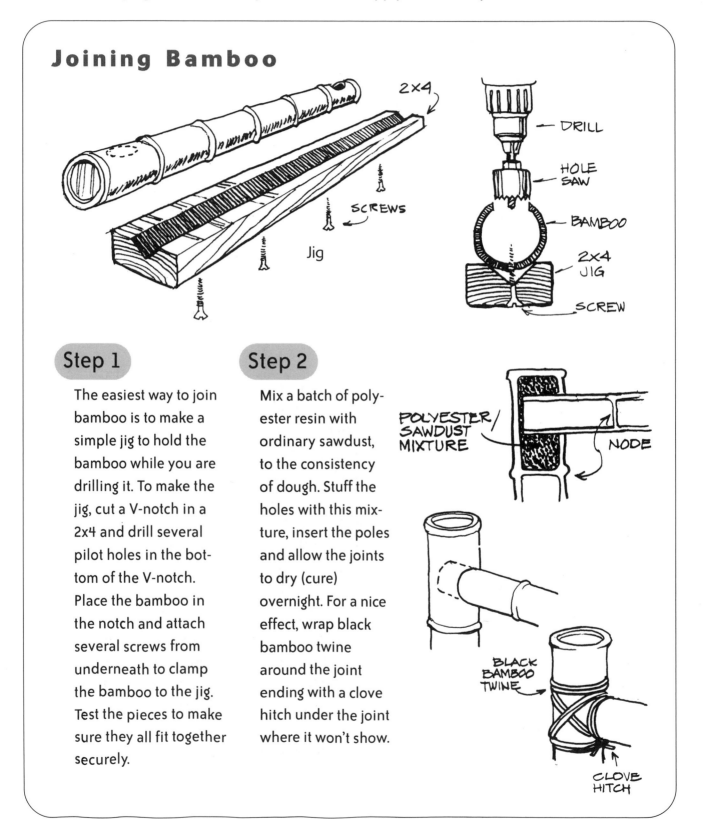

Step 1

The easiest way to join bamboo is to make a simple jig to hold the bamboo while you are drilling it. To make the jig, cut a V-notch in a 2x4 and drill several pilot holes in the bottom of the V-notch. Place the bamboo in the notch and attach several screws from underneath to clamp the bamboo to the jig. Test the pieces to make sure they all fit together securely.

Step 2

Mix a batch of polyester resin with ordinary sawdust, to the consistency of dough. Stuff the holes with this mixture, insert the poles and allow the joints to dry (cure) overnight. For a nice effect, wrap black bamboo twine around the joint ending with a clove hitch under the joint where it won't show.

Decking

Standard decking used in house construction is normally listed as $5/4$x4 or $5/4$x6 pressure-treated lumber or cedar that is rot resistant. The term $5/4$ means that the board measures about 1 inch thick as opposed to the more common board that is $3/4$ inch thick. Each board is spaced about $1/8$ inch apart. Many professional house builders use a 16d nail to temporarily space the boards apart while they are screwing them down. The deck boards are held down by coated, square drive deck screws and rest on floor joists, spaced either 16 or 24 inches apart.

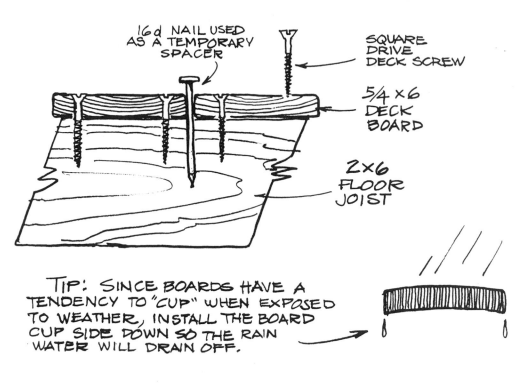

16d NAIL USED AS A TEMPORARY SPACER

SQUARE DRIVE DECK SCREW

$5/4 \times 6$ DECK BOARD

2×6 FLOOR JOIST

TIP: SINCE BOARDS HAVE A TENDENCY TO "CUP" WHEN EXPOSED TO WEATHER, INSTALL THE BOARD CUP SIDE DOWN SO THE RAIN WATER WILL DRAIN OFF.

Floor decking

One type of flooring worth considering is 2x6 tongue and groove (T&G) fir decking, often used in barns. Its advantage is that it can span 4 feet without a support, making fewer floor joists necessary. This is a solid type of decking and is best used on the interior of the treehouse.

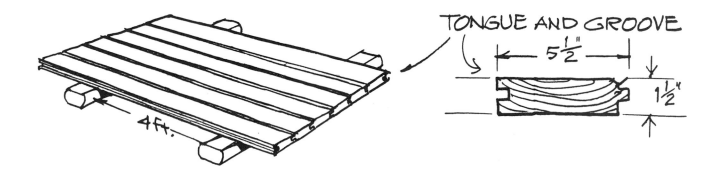

4ft.

TONGUE AND GROOVE

$5\frac{1}{2}$"

$1\frac{1}{2}$"

Staging or Scaffolding Planks

Another useful tip is to buy boards used by carpenters and painters for scaffolding and to use this (instead of standard lumber) for decking. These boards, 2 inches thick and 9 inches wide, come 13 feet long. Their advantage is that they can span greater distances than regular lumber. This means they only need to be supported in two places, eliminating the need for building a floor frame with multiple floor joists. This is especially helpful in a tree where it is difficult to find more than two branches at the same level. These boards are purposely left with a rough surface so that they won't be slippery underfoot, however, a light sanding may be necessary to eliminate splinters.

Spans

The word "span" refers to the distance that a beam, log or board can go between two supports and still hold the intended load. Engineers use this term when they are designing bridges and are challenged to build a bridge with the maximum span.

In treehouse construction, spans are important because you don't want to build a floor that sags in the middle or runs the risk of breaking. A lot depends on the thickness and size of the lumber and how it is laid on the supports.

For example, a rule of thumb in treehouse construction:

✳ Treehouse Span Table

A 1x4 laid flat can span 12 inches (when used as a floorboard).

A 1x6 laid flat can span 16 inches (when used as a floorboard).

A 2x4 laid flat can span 24 inches (when used as a floorboard) or 36 inches if laid on edge to be used as a support beam.

A 2x6 laid flat can span 36 inches (when used as a floorboard) or 6 feet if laid on edge to be used as a support beam.

A 2x8 laid flat can span 48 inches (when used as a floorboard) or 8 feet if laid on edge to be used as a support beam.

A 2x10 laid flat can span 5 feet (when used as a floorboard) or 10 feet if used on edge as a support beam.

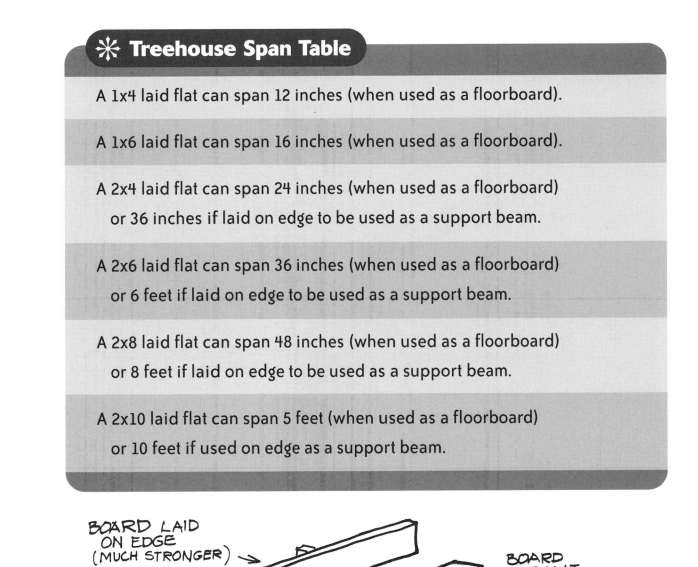

BOARD LAID ON EDGE (MUCH STRONGER)

BOARD LAID FLAT

SPAN

Lumber Delivery

If you are having your lumber delivered, tell the lumber company where to drop it and mark the spot on your property with a sign. It's a good idea to lay down skids (boards) for the lumber to rest on. We have seen termites attack lumber that has been lying on the ground for only a few days. Leave a tarp for them to cover it with.

Making a Simple Sawhorse

This sawhorse, made from ³/₄-inch plywood and 2x6 lumber, is designed specifically for kids and is a valuable aid for building many of the projects in this book. It is not easy for kids to accurately saw through a piece of lumber. To make it easier, build this simple sawhorse using these directions.

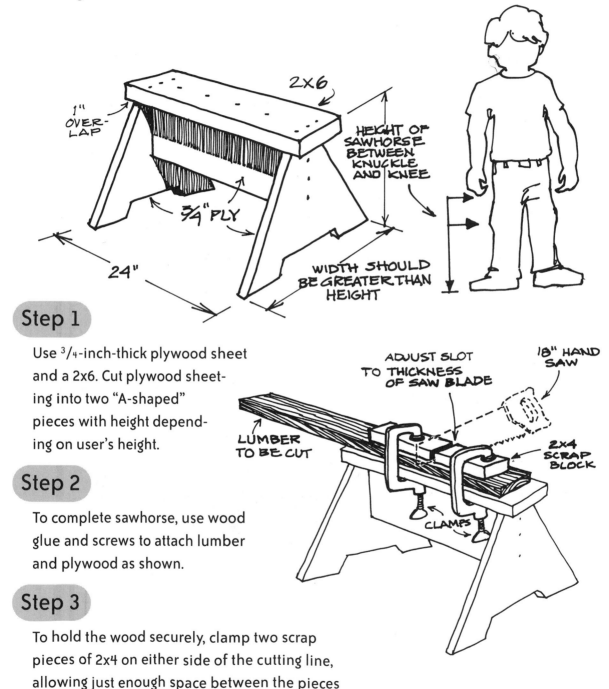

Step 1

Use ³/₄-inch-thick plywood sheet and a 2x6. Cut plywood sheeting into two "A-shaped" pieces with height depending on user's height.

Step 2

To complete sawhorse, use wood glue and screws to attach lumber and plywood as shown.

Step 3

To hold the wood securely, clamp two scrap pieces of 2x4 on either side of the cutting line, allowing just enough space between the pieces (about ¹/₁₆ inch) for the saw blade to fit through.

Sawing Through Lumber

No

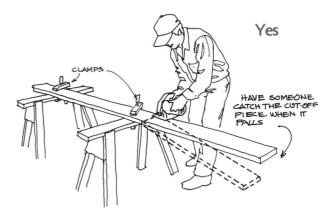

Yes

CLAMPS

HAVE SOMEONE CATCH THE CUT-OFF PIECE WHEN IT FALLS

When lumber is cut between two supports, it will bind and the saw blade can "kick back."

Instead, clamp the lumber to the sawhorses and cut outside the supports so the piece being cut off will fall away, without binding.

Bolts, Nails and Screws

When building any project that will be kept outdoors, make sure that the bolts, nuts, washers, nails, and screws are galvanized or have some kind of protective coating. The only exception is rust-resistant stainless steel.

Bolts

Lag bolts are often called lag screws.

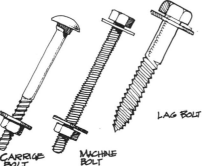

CARRIAGE BOLT

MACHINE BOLT

LAG BOLT

Finishing Nails

Finishing nails are used in finished carpentry where the nail heads hardly show.

$2\frac{1}{2}$"

2"

$1\frac{1}{2}$"

Deck Screws

Deck screws are sold as either Phillips-head screws or square-drive screws.

Common Nails

Common nails are still referred to and sold as "d" or "penny" nails.

The following nails are good to have in stock:

16d–$3\frac{1}{2}$ inches long for heavy framing
10d–3 inches long for light framing
6d–2 inches long for siding
3d–$1\frac{1}{2}$ inches long for roofing

"Secret" Glue

Quite often it becomes necessary to strengthen a joint, fill a hole, or glue two pieces of wood together. Many products claim to do all these things, but these are the ones we have found to work best.

Construction Adhesives

There are two manufacturers of polyurethane construction adhesives: *PL* and *Liquid Nails*. Polyurethane adhesives that come in tubes or cartridges can be used to help join beams to a tree. Some of the cartridge guns have an easy

was invented to fix bumps in cars. It is used more and more by carpenters who have recently discovered it. To use it, find a piece of stiff cardboard and scoop out a glob of Bondo onto it. Squeeze out a tiny bit of hardener and mix the two together with a putty knife. Apply it quickly as you have only about 5 to 10 minutes before it completely hardens. It can then be carved out or sanded smooth. The color ends up being a grayish pinkish brown. Make sure to read the warning label, wear a mask, and do the work outside.

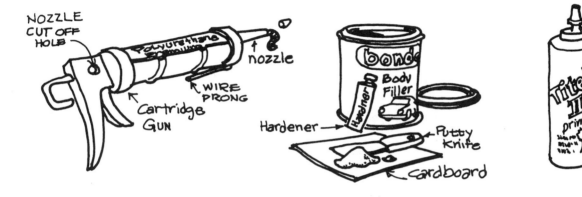

way of cutting off the tip of the nozzle by placing it in a hole above the handle. Use the wire prong attached to the gun to unseal the adhesive inside the nozzle. This glue dries quickly (about 30 minutes), but needs 24 hours to reach maximum strength. The nice thing about it is that it is the same color as pressure-treated wood. Be careful not to get any on your skin as it quickly sticks, and you will need to use paint thinner *immediately* to remove it. It covers gaps up to $3/8$ inch wide and is great for covering up mistakes.

Auto Body Filler

Forget all other wood fillers—this inexpensive product is the one we like the best. Bondo Auto Body Filler with 2.750Z hardener *(see Resources)*

Yellow Glue

The only glue that comes close to being waterproof is Titebond III. Make sure it is Titebond III as the Titebond Original is only water resistant, not waterproof. This is great for making small repairs, gluing pegs, or sealing splinters. If you use it on a large area, make sure both surfaces are completely covered so that they "suck" together. If possible, hold the pieces together using clamps. It should take 30 minutes to dry and 24 hours to reach maximum strength.

> **Note:**
>
> Make sure to read all instructions and warnings on glue labels.

Installing Posts

Using posts to support a treehouse has many advantages. A treehouse supported by posts is lower to the ground and easier to build. It is also not affected by the wind that can sway a treehouse built high up in the tree, therefore, you will not need to construct flexible joints to allow for tree movement.

Use posts that are longer than you need. Cut them to the correct height after the structure has been framed. Whenever possible, design the posts to become part of the structure. For example, allow the post to support the floor AND the railing.

Step 1

Before installing the posts, coat the bottoms with roofing cement (tar), continuing the tar 6 to 8 inches above the point where the post emerges from the ground. This will protect the post from snow and rain that can cause rot.

Step 2

Dig a hole several inches wider than the post. You will ALWAYS need to adjust the posts sideways one way or another. Dig the hole at least 30 inches into the ground or below the frost line. Tamp down the bottom of the hole with a 2x4 and place a flat rock or brick on the bottom of the hole for the post to stand on.

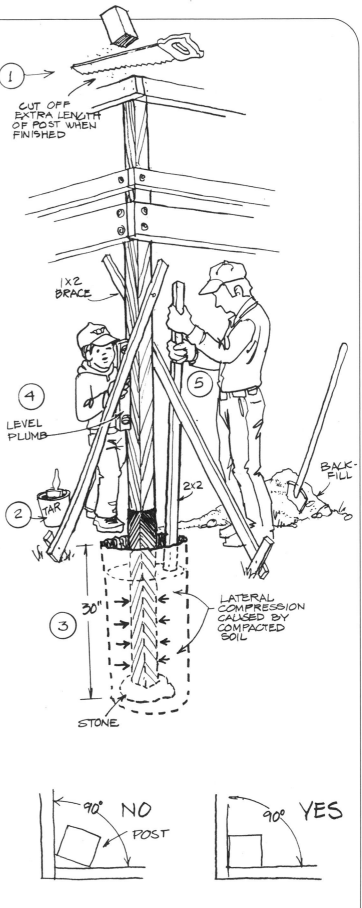

① CUT OFF EXTRA LENGTH OF POST WHEN FINISHED

1x2 BRACE

④ LEVEL PLUMB

⑤

② TAR

③ 30"

2x2

BACK-FILL

LATERAL COMPRESSION CAUSED BY COMPACTED SOIL

STONE

90° NO POST

90° YES

Step 3

The posts must be plumb (vertical) on two adjacent sides and square to each other. The easiest way to do this is to attach the beams temporarily to the posts while the posts are standing loosely in their holes. Once they are correctly aligned, hold them in place with diagonal braces while you backfill the holes.

Step 4

Backfill the holes by adding one shovelful of soil at a time and tamping it down HARD with a 2x2 pole before adding the next shovelful. This is best done by two people—one adding the soil and one tamping it down forcefully. If the soil is tamped down hard enough, there is no need to use concrete since it is the force of the lateral compression of the soil that keeps the post from pulling out of the ground.

Making Concrete Footings

If the ground where you want to place the post is bedrock, you can still install a post.

Step 1

Drill a $1/2$-inch-diameter hole 8 to 10 inches deep into the rock using a masonry drill. Partially fill the hole with thin-set cement and insert a $1/2$-inch-diameter by 10-inch-long eyebolt into the hole. For added strength, place a bolt through the eye of the eyebolt.

Step 2

Take a 12-inch-diameter by 14-inch-long piece of cardboard tubing called "Sonatube" and cut the bottom of the tube to fit the shape of the rock surface. Place the Sonatube over the eyebolt, seal the bottom around the Sonatube with cement and allow it to cure overnight.

Step 3

Hammer some nails into the bottom of the post to help hold it in the concrete. Place the post in the Sonatube and after it is carefully aligned and braced, fill it with concrete.

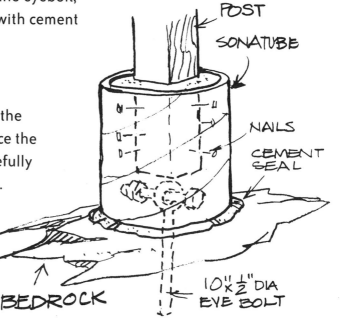

POST

SONATUBE

NAILS

CEMENT SEAL

BEDROCK

$10" \times \frac{1}{2}"$ DIA EYE BOLT

Rope Railings

Rope railings give a treehouse the "shipwreck" look inspired by the tale of Robinson Caruso, who built a home in a tree from salvaged wood after his ship wrecked on a deserted island (which incidentally is based on a true story).

To make a rope railing, it is best to use round poles for the horizontal rails rather than square lumber so that the rope will wrap around the rails naturally. We use ¹/₂-inch manila hemp rope for this job. Do not use yellow polypropylene rope that will deteriorate in the sun.

Check the label on the rope to make sure it does not say "biodegradable" since this type of rope is designed to rot in a few years. You can use nylon or Dacron rope but it is rather expensive and the white color does not look best for a treehouse.

Making Rope Railings

Step 1

To tie the rope to the railing, start by boring a ⁵/₈-inch-diameter hole 2 inches deep into one of the posts just under the top rail. Fill the hole partway with construction adhesive *(see "Secret" Glue, page 28)* and insert one end of the ¹/₂-inch rope. Secure it with a 2-inch galvanized screw driven at an angle through the rope. The construction adhesive will expand in a few hours and fill the difference between the ¹/₂-inch rope and the ⁵/₈-inch hole.

Step 2

Feed the coil of rope under and over and "catch" it behind itself before bringing it down and around to form the next loop. Continue making loops until you reach the other side, then bring the rope down to the bottom rail and make loops back to the first post. Secure the end of the rope the same way as in Step 1.

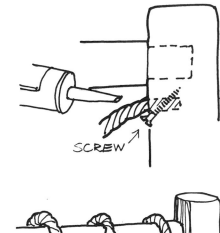

SCREW

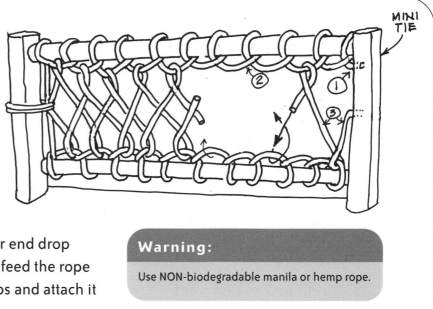

Step 3

Make another $^5/_8$-inch hole halfway down the post and attach another rope to it. Feed this rope through every other loop, once again, making sure to catch it behind itself before proceeding. When you have reached the other end drop down to the lower rail and feed the rope through the remaining loops and attach it to the post as in Step 1.

Warning:

Use NON-biodegradable manila or hemp rope.

Branch Rails

One alternative to rope railing is to fit Y-shaped branches made out of cedar or hickory between the rails. Find interesting pieces of wood with gnarls and burls that give it personality. Fit one end of each branch into a drilled out hole in the rail. Attach the opposite ends using pegs or screws.

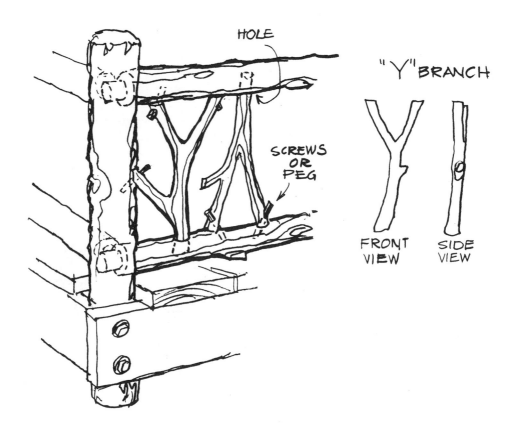

Doors

Doors should be made in "kid-proportions." Although we don't think they need to be made high enough for adults to walk through standing upright, we suggest building them no shorter than 4 feet high and no less than 2 feet wide so adults can still enter. Wooden door latches and slide bolts are suitable for treehouses and playhouse doors. They are also easy to make.

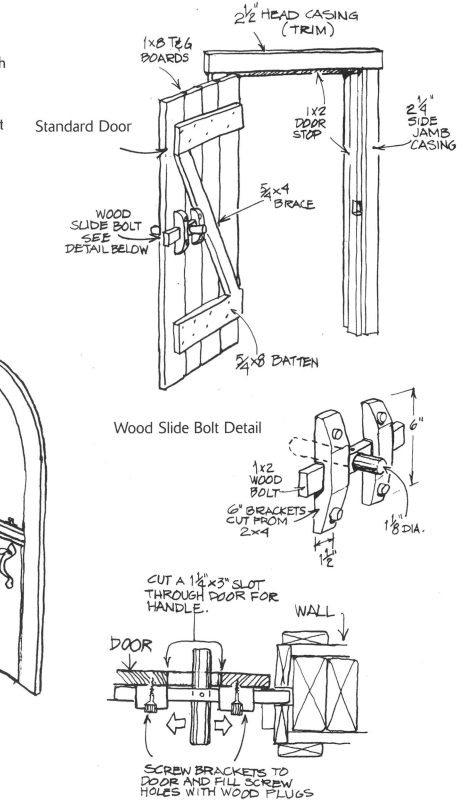

Standard Door

2½" HEAD CASING (TRIM)

1x8 T&G BOARDS

1x2 DOOR STOP

2¼" SIDE JAMB CASING

5/4 x 4 BRACE

WOOD SLIDE BOLT SEE DETAIL BELOW

5/4 x 8 BATTEN

Wood Slide Bolt Detail

6"

1x2 WOOD BOLT

6" BRACKETS CUT FROM 2x4

1⅛" DIA.

1½"

CUT A 1¼" x 3" SLOT THROUGH DOOR FOR HANDLE.

DOOR

WALL

SCREW BRACKETS TO DOOR AND FILL SCREW HOLES WITH WOOD PLUGS

Top View Plan of Slide Bolt

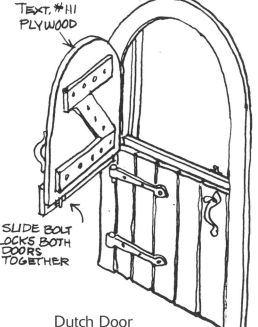

TEXT. #H1 PLYWOOD

SLIDE BOLT LOCKS BOTH DOORS TOGETHER

Dutch Door

Easy-to-Make Plexiglas Window

This window takes only thirty minutes to make. Because it is made out of Plexiglas or acrylic sheeting, it will not break or shatter if a branch falls on it or if a bully is trying to get your attention!

Step 1

Cut an opening for the window to the size that you want, then cut a piece of $3/4$-inch plywood, $1/8$ inch shorter on all sides (to allow for clearance). Cut the inside holes for the window using an electric jigsaw. You can cut the corners square, but making them rounded (as shown here) is easier and may even look better.

Step 2

Cut a piece of $1/2$-inch Plexiglas the same size as the plywood. Drill pilot holes slightly larger than the screws to allow for expansion and contraction of the plastic and screw the plastic to the back (interior side) of the plywood window. Attach two hinges to the window and to the outside wall of the treehouse or playhouse.

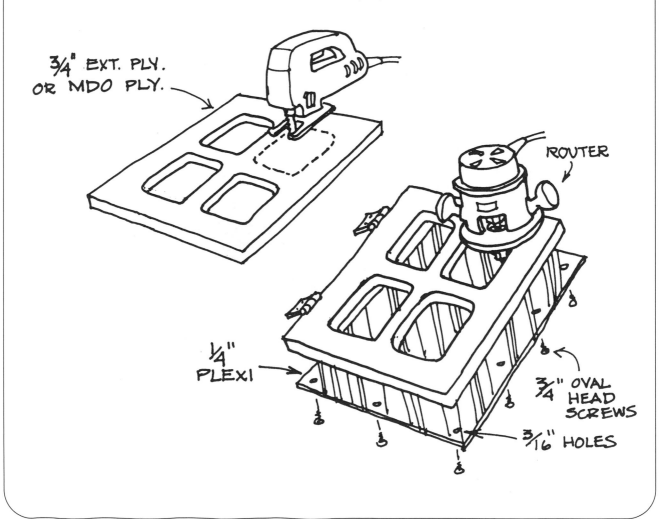

Attaching a Window

You can find used windows at your local dump or order inexpensive plastic windows *(see Resources)*. Make sure you get the windows BEFORE you frame the walls of your tree-house, so that you can leave the correct amount of space between the studs. The studs and the wall siding should be $1/2$ inch shorter on both sides than the opening so that the window closes against the siding, which acts as a stop.

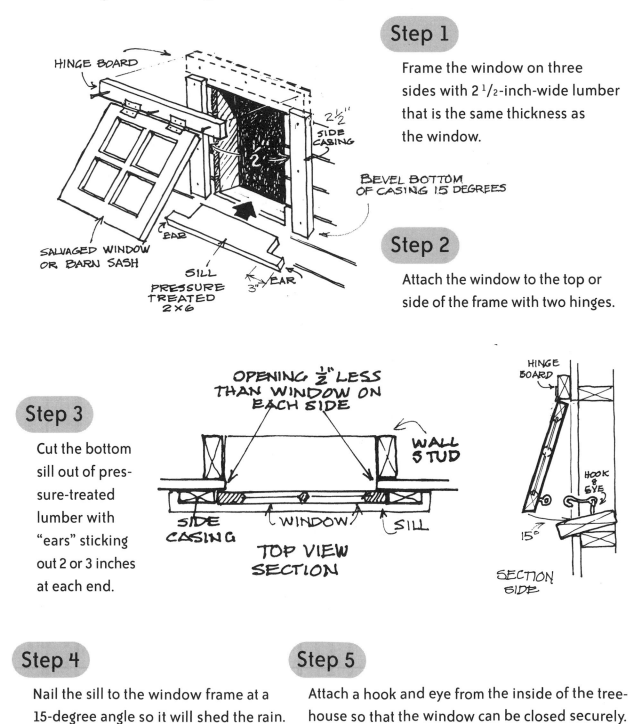

Step 1

Frame the window on three sides with 2 $1/2$-inch-wide lumber that is the same thickness as the window.

Step 2

Attach the window to the top or side of the frame with two hinges.

Step 3

Cut the bottom sill out of pressure-treated lumber with "ears" sticking out 2 or 3 inches at each end.

Step 4

Nail the sill to the window frame at a 15-degree angle so it will shed the rain.

Step 5

Attach a hook and eye from the inside of the tree-house so that the window can be closed securely.

Skylights

Many treehouses suffer from not enough light inside. A simple way to solve this problem is to include a skylight in your design when you are framing the roof. A skylight not only lights up the interior space, but also gives treehouse dwellers another view, looking up through tree branches into the sky and stargazing at night.

Building a Simple Fixed Skylight

Step 1

Nail two crosspieces between two rafters to form a box. Nail the sheathing boards onto the rafters, leaving out the section where the skylight will be uncovered.

CROSS PIECES

RAFTERS

Step 2

Cut a piece of $1/8$-inch Plexiglas, 2 inches larger than the hole, on all sides.

Step 3

Glue the Plexiglas to the sheathing, using clear silicone caulking. While the caulking is still wet, slip a piece of aluminum flashing or tar paper under the bottom edge of the Plexiglas.

Step 4

$\frac{1}{8}$" PLEXI

ROOF SHEATHING BOARDS

ALUM. OR TAR PAPER FLASHING

SHINGLES OR ROLL ROOFING

Use asphalt shingles or roll roofing to cover the roof. Slip the roofing material under the aluminum flashing at the bottom of the skylight and continue adding the roofing, applying silicone caulking at the edges where the roofing material overlaps the Plexiglas. Be sure to overlap the top edge of the Plexiglas with roofing material by at least 2 inches.

Building an Operable Skylight

Sometimes it's nice to have a skylight that can open so you can get some fresh air, or so that you can climb out on the roof or up into the tree.

Step 1

To make an operable skylight, you need to build a "curb" on top of the roof. This can be a simple box frame made up of 2x3s the same inside dimension as the hole. Nail the curb to the roof.

Step 2

Cut a piece of $1/2$-inch-thick Plexiglas so that it overlaps the box frame curb by $1/2$ inch on three sides. Attach the Plexiglas to the top of the curb using two hinges. Use small bolts to attach the hinges to the Plexiglas and flat head screws to attach the hinges to the top of the curb.

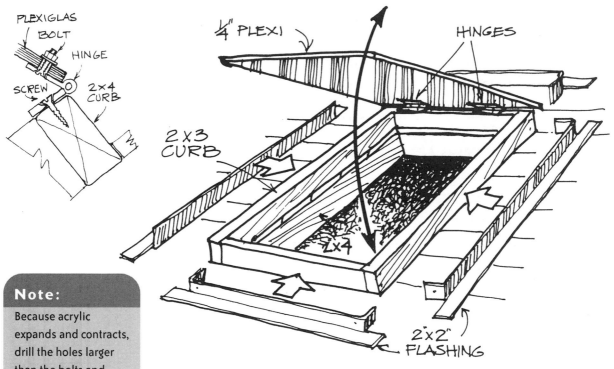

PLEXIGLAS
BOLT
HINGE
SCREW
2x4 CURB

$\frac{1}{4}$" PLEXI

HINGES

2X3 CURB

2X4

2"X2" FLASHING

Note:
Because acrylic expands and contracts, drill the holes larger than the bolts and screws so that there is some "wiggle room."

Step 3

Before adding your final roofing material, attach 2x2-inch flashing, sold in most lumber-yards, as "roof edging" to the curb where it meets the roof. Use plenty of silicone caulking and as few nails as possible to hold the flashing in place before applying the final roofing material or shingles.

Building a Loft

If you plan on building a loft or sleeping platform in the front of your treehouse or playhouse, it may be necessary to increase the slant of the roof to provide enough head room for the loft. It's also a good idea to add a window or opening in the loft area, for ventilation and a view.

Step 1

You will need to make the tree or playhouse door opening as low as possible to allow more headroom in the loft. Typical dimensions are shown here, but you should adjust these according to the size of the kids using the house. This may make your tree or playhouse as tall as 7 or 8 feet. One alternative is to build the loft in the back of the house, unencumbered by the front door, and to slant the roof the other way.

Step 2

Use a ladder to access your loft and provide a 12-inch-high safety rail.

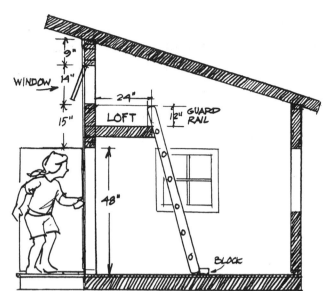

* DIMENSIONS SHOWN ARE HYPOTHETICAL AND SHOULD BE ADJUSTED TO SUIT YOUR SITUATION.

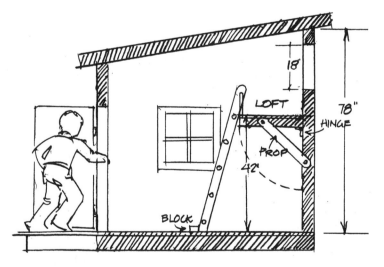

> **Note:**
>
> Planning the interior of the house is important. Use grid paper and make plans showing where all the furniture, etc., will go before you begin construction. For example, you could have the loft platform supported by props and attached by hinges that swing down when not in use; or you could have it suspended from chains, attached to the ceiling, that can be hoisted up using pulleys.

Construction Abbreviations and Symbols

( ) = QUANTITY

& = AND

′ = FEET

″ = INCHES

O.C. = ON CENTER

℄ = CENTER LINE

DIA = DIAMETER

R. = RADIUS

EXT. = EXTERIOR

TEXT. = TEXTURE

ELEVATION = VIEW OF A SIDE

PLAN = VIEW LOOKING DOWN

R.O. = ROUGH OPENING FOR WINDOWS & DOORS

∅ = DIAMETER

GALV. = GALVANIZED (COATING)

T&G = TONGUE IN GROOVE

W/ = WITH

FTG. = FOOTING

⊠ = SECTION OF LUMBER

▱ = BLOCKING BETWEEN LUMBER.

▭ = CUT - LUMBER

▱ = CUT - PIPE OR TUBING

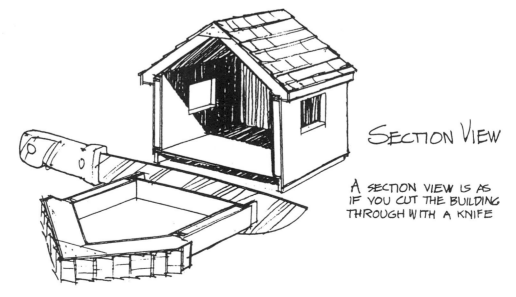

SECTION VIEW

A SECTION VIEW IS AS
IF YOU CUT THE BUILDING
THROUGH WITH A KNIFE

Choose a spot that:

1. Can be reached by an electric extension cord.

2. Isn't visible from a neighbor's house.

3. Is within reach of building supplies.

4. Has at least one good tree to build in.

BUILDING A TREEHOUSE

*"There is no greater feeling than to be
Perched way high up in a tree."*
—David Stiles

Few words can accurately explain the feeling of being up in a tree, but there is a definite sense of being somewhere exciting and different.

A proper treehouse looks like a kid built it even if he didn't. There has been a trend recently to build "adult" treehouses exactly the way real houses are built by professional house builders. We feel this eliminates the fantasy element of treehouses that began when the first kid decided to nail a few boards up in a tree and make it his or her own special hideaway home.

Remember, a treehouse is for kids. It should be their domain, their private place, their sanctuary and their responsibility to keep clean and to play in safely. If you're lucky, they will let you come up for a visit once in a while. If you build them a treehouse and grant them sole ownership, you will also be building them wonderful memories they will never forget.

Building a treehouse takes a lot of careful thought, creativity, and ingenuity. If you happen to be professional house builders (as we are) you may find that your skills and experience in building perfectly rectangular houses is of little use in building a treehouse. In fact, you may be on par with the novice weekend carpenter who has no building experience at all. What is really necessary is having an open mind to all the possibilities of joining wood to trees in a manner that is sufficiently strong to withstand future windstorms and invasions by neighborhood kids.

Since every tree is different, it is impossible to draw up an exact set of plans and expect to have them fit every tree. You can, however, by referring to this book, find a solution to most of the sticky problems you are likely to encounter while building a treehouse. The most important thing is to have a good idea of where and how the main supports will go. Once they are solidly in place, you are ready to move forward.

When you are figuring out construction details, imagine you are Robinson Caruso or a Native American living during a time when hardware and lumber stores were not available. You'll be surprised how many construction problems can be solved just using your own ingenuity. And, you may also save yourself an unnecessary trip to town.

Family Meeting

Call a family meeting—perhaps on a Saturday morning when everyone has come to breakfast. Ask everyone at the meeting to make a "wish list." Discuss what type of treehouse (or playhouse) will fulfill all your personal dreams and wishes. Consider how the treehouse will look in the winter when the leaves are missing, and perhaps equally important, how it will look from your neighbor's house.

Take several photos from different angles of the tree or building site where you plan to build. Lay a piece of tracing paper or acetate over the photograph and sketch your idea for the structure from different points of view *(see Figure 1)*.

Try to situate your structure in a place where it will not be visible by neighbors and, if possible, keep it set back from your property line. Show your designs to your neighbors, apologize in advance for the noise you will be making and perhaps even bring cookies as compensation. (This is actually done in Japan on large construction projects.) Most neighbors will appreciate your consideration and give the project their blessing, leaving you with the peace of mind to go ahead with construction. You may even want to ask for their suggestions (you don't have to take them). Remind them that a tree or playhouse is a "temporary play structure," not an "accessory building," controlled by building codes, and will eventually be removed.

Planning a Treehouse

Step 1

Take a photo of the site.

Step 2

Make a pen-and-ink sketch of the treehouse on a piece of clear acetate laid over the photo.

Step 3

Apply paint to the back of the clear acetate.

Step 4

Lay acetate overlay over the photo to illustrate how the treehouse will look when it is built.

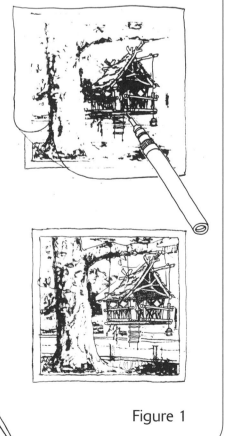

Figure 1

Planned Building vs. Building as You Go

There are two basic ways to build a treehouse: planned building or building as you go. "Planned building" is when you have a situation where you can use predetermined plans. Most of the materials and dimensions are listed and all you have to do is follow the step-by-step instructions. This is preferred by most home-owners since it takes the least amount of time to build the treehouse and reduces the amount of problem solving and head scratching. This type of treehouse is built closer to the ground, some-times using posts to support it. Because it is close to the ground, it is less dangerous and more easily accessible for kids to play in it. Materials for this type of treehouse are often more expensive because they are bought at a lumberyard and delivered to your house.

"Building as you go" is when you have no exact plans, just a desire to build something in the trees where you can sit and contemplate the universe. You might begin by climbing into the tree and attaching two strong support beams to the tree, using rope pulleys (blocks) to tem-porarily hold them in place while you work. Treehouses like this are usually built higher up in the branches of the tree and quite often use salvaged wood. Even though they are built in an ad-hoc manner, they must still be built strong and with a level platform (something young treehouse builders tend to forget). This type of treehouse builder is more adventuresome and needs to be able to solve problems as they come up. To help these intrepid builders, we have included several pages of the book to problems that arise when "free building" in a tree and a choice of solutions.

One of these problems is how to attach a beam to a tree that has grown at unpredictable angles. Another is how to attach a beam to branches that will always be moving in the wind. We have spent years analyzing these problems and hope the suggestions we have illustrated in this book will be of some help to those deciding to build without plans or higher up in the tree.

Choosing the Right Tree

A treehouse can be built in almost any tree as long as the tree is healthy, sturdy, and sufficiently strong to support the weight of the building materials and the occupants (see Figure 2). Our favorite types of trees for building a treehouse are Banyans, Cottonwoods, Beech or any large sprawling trees like Elms and Maples. The per-fect tree would be 3 to 4 feet in diameter with large horizontal branches 8 to 10 feet from the ground. The only trees that we do not recom-mend are trees with shallow roots, like birches, or palm trees that bend and sway in the wind.

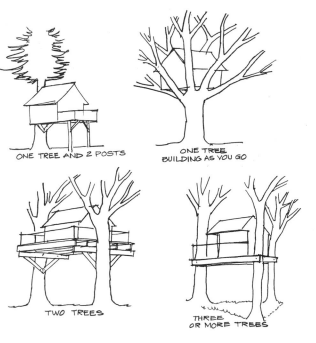

Figure 2

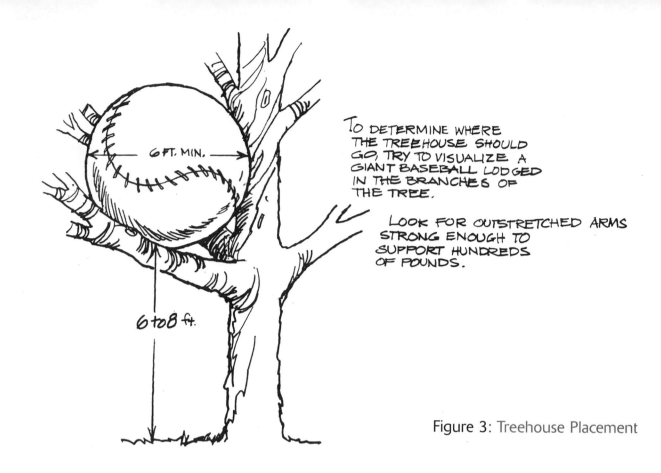

To determine where the treehouse should go, try to visualize a giant baseball lodged in the branches of the tree.

Look for outstretched arms strong enough to support hundreds of pounds.

6 ft. min.

6 to 8 ft.

Figure 3: Treehouse Placement

If you are relying on tree branches alone to support the treehouse, the branches should be at least 6 to 8 inches thick where they join the tree. If, like most people, you do not have a perfect tree to build in, you can use a small tree as the main support and add two posts for additional support. You can also build a treehouse between two or three small trees; however, it may be necessary to provide some sort of flexible or sliding joint where the beams join the trees since the trees will be moving independently of each other in the wind *(see page 47)*.

In your mind's eye, try to visualize where a giant baseball could go *(see Figure 3)*. Look for outstretched arms strong enough to support hundreds of pounds. If possible, position the treehouse so that it has a nice view. Get a ladder, climb up into the tree and take a look around. While you are up there, take measurements of the distances between branches and write them down. A parent once told us one of the best moments he ever experienced with his child was spent just sitting in a tree, planning how they were going to build their treehouse.

Height of the Treehouse

Most kids' treehouses are built 7 to 8 feet off the ground so you will be able to construct the floor frame while standing on the ground. This still gives you the feeling of being high up in the air that makes being in a treehouse so exciting.

Treehouse Maintenance

It's a good idea to check your treehouse after a storm and make any necessary repairs. When spring arrives, sweep out any fall leaves and insects that might have moved in over the winter. Check to make sure that all ropes, joints, floorboards, and stairs are safe and secure.

Tree Expansion and Movement

Every year trees grow taller, the ends of the branches reaching out to the sun for light. As a treehouse builder, however, you should also take into consideration that the tree trunk grows in circumference and diameter *(see Figure 4)*. The rate of growth depends on the species of tree and the growing conditions in a particular year. A wet spring means the tree will grow more. An average tree trunk grows about $1/8$ inch in width a year. The growth can be seen in the rings of a cross section of a tree. This is not a big problem if you want your treehouse to last only a few years. If, however, you want your grandchildren to be playing in the treehouse 15 to 20 years from now, you will need to take a few precautions.

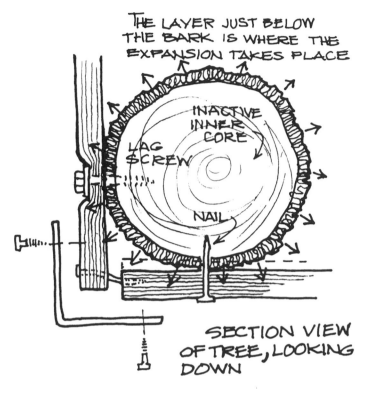

THE LAYER JUST BELOW THE BARK IS WHERE THE EXPANSION TAKES PLACE

INACTIVE INNER CORE

LAG SCREW

NAIL

SECTION VIEW OF TREE, LOOKING DOWN

Figure 4: Expansion

As a tree trunk expands, any beams held by nails will gradually be pushed out from the tree *(see Figure 4)*. Beams held by lag screws, however, will remain imbedded in the tree, held by their coarse threads. After a few years, you may notice that the lag screws appear to have been sucked into the beam. To prevent them from being pulled all the way through the beam, use a socket wrench to back off the screw, half a turn, every one or two years. On the other hand, you may find, after five or ten years, that the tree has actually grown around the beam making the joint even stronger.

After several years, the tree growth can also force joints apart *(see Figure 5)*. These should be repaired using heavy metal corner brackets or, in some cases, by replacing the beam altogether.

CORNER BRACKET

Figure 5: Corner Bracket Detail

If the trunk of your tree is over 1 foot in diameter and you are building your treehouse platform close to the ground, the wind will have very little effect on the treehouse. The tree branches at the top of a tree, however, can move as much as 2 feet in either direction *(see Figure 6)*. This is one reason why it is problematic to build high up in a tree.

To determine how much two trees swayed over a period of a year, we attached a beam to two 5-inch-diameter trees, 6 feet up in the air, and found that the trees moved $^1/_2$ inch in all directions. If we had attached the beam higher in the tree, the movement would have been even greater.

If a board is attached to two trees, some allowance should be made at one end of the beam for a flexible connection so the trees can move with the wind *(see Figure 8 on page 47)*.

The reason only one lag screw (bolt) is put into each tree is to allow for this movement. The bolt acts as a pivot point, allowing the platform to remain level as the tree bends. This design is based on the "parallelogram" that you learn about in high school geometry class *(see Figure 6)*. If you use two bolts in each tree, restricting the movement of the two trees, the force of resistance can be too great, causing the bolts to split the end of the boards *(see Figure 7)*.

When a beam is attached to two trees, over a period of five to ten years the beam may favor one tree (the one that has the tightest connection). The tree with the stronger connection can begin to grow around the beam, encasing it, making a very strong joint. If this happens, the joint on the other end of the beam should be allowed to move and should be checked every

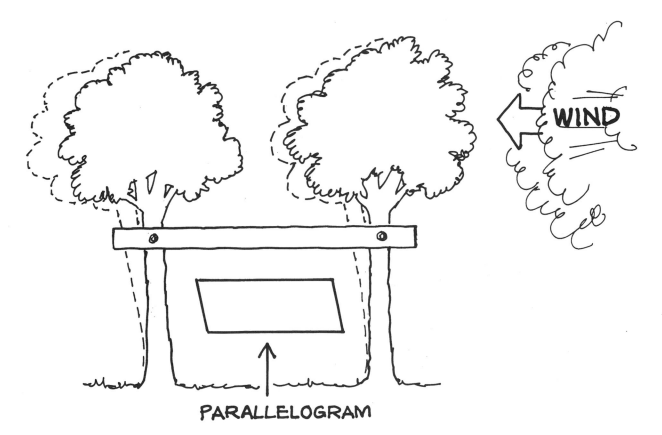

WIND

PARALLELOGRAM

Figure 6

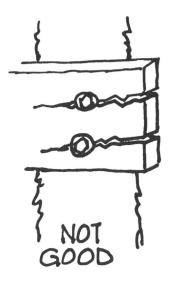

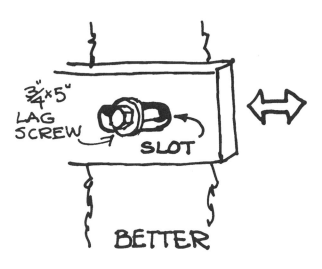

Figure 7: No Movement Allowed

Figure 8: Movement Allowed

year. If both connections are fixed, one of them can break (shear), especially if the lag screw measures less than $1/2$ inch in diameter.

One easy solution, if you don't anticipate much tree movement, is to have the lag screw fit through a slotted hole in the beam, made by drilling two holes and chiseling out the material between them *(see Figure 8).* That way the beam rides back and forth on the lag screw, allowing for some movement. For this connection, use an extra heavy $3/4$-inch-diameter lag screw and embed it at least 4 inches into the tree. Resist the temptation to tighten the lag screw so the beam can't move. On the contrary, you may even need to back off (unscrew) the lag screw each year as the tree expands in circumference. Make sure to inspect all connections each year for safety.

If you are building high in the tree, you should also consider using flexible connections. Use strong support beams, attached to the tree with $1/2$- to $3/4$-inch-diameter bolts in each joint. Allow a little room for the tree to expand by making the pilot hole slightly larger than the

diameter of the lag screw. Use only one bolt (lag screw) in each joint so the trees can sway together *(see Figure 6).* As you can see from our sketch, the beam remains level even when the trees are bent over. There are several other ways to allow for tree movement. *(See Flexible Connections on pages 49–51.)*

If you build your treehouse in one tree, using its trunk as your only support, you don't need to make a flexible connection. The treehouse will move in unison with the tree. If, however, you attach part of the treehouse to branches, make the branch connections flexible.

If you build a treehouse high up in the trees in a windy area, make sure your floor platform is secured in a flexible way, allowing the treehouse to "float" *(see Flexible Connections pages 49–51).* Use substantial support beams that are securely attached to the tree. Or you can suspend your treehouse from ropes attached to branches above.

Installing a Lag Screw

Attaching a beam to a tree using a lag screw isn't as easy as it looks. It's important to take your time and do it correctly *(see Figure 9)*. A lag screw should be no less than $1/2$ inch in diameter for spans up to 6 feet. Use a larger screw for longer spans. Make sure at least 3 inches of the lag screw is embedded in the tree.

Step 1

Drill a hole in the beam that is a tiny bit larger in diameter than the lag screw.

Step 2

Use this hole to mark the tree by pushing a pencil or marker through the hole. **Make sure the beam is level first.**

Step 3

Drill a pilot hole into the tree using a drill that is smaller than the threads on the screw.

Step 4

Hold the beam in position (sometimes with a rope attached to a tree limb above) and hammer the lag screw through the beam and into the tree.

Step 5

Use a socket wrench to turn the lag screw $1/2$ turn.

Step 6

Strike the lag screw head HARD with a hammer and give the screw $1/2$ turn. At this point you might be tempted to just screw the lag screw all the way in without hitting it with the hammer— DON'T! *(See following note.)*

Step 7

Repeat this procedure four or five times until you are sure the screw is well started and the threads have taken hold in the tree. If your tree is very hard it may be necessary to slide a length of pipe onto the end of the wrench to gain more leverage. Then screw it all the way in until you see the washer squeeze into the wood of the tree beam.

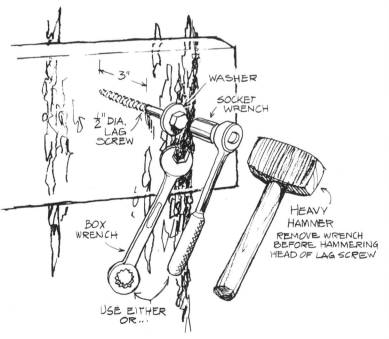

3"

WASHER

SOCKET WRENCH

$1/2$" DIA. LAG SCREW

BOX WRENCH

HEAVY HAMMER

REMOVE WRENCH BEFORE HAMMERING HEAD OF LAG SCREW

USE EITHER OR...

Figure 9

Note:

This is important because if you don't get the lag screw threads biting sufficiently into the tree, there is a chance that the threads could "strip" and pull out. You'll know if you have done it right if there is a lot of resistance when you turn the socket wrench during the last turns.

Split-Level Play Decks

Nina and Lily Patricof enjoy playing on these two decks with rope railings that make up phase one of the Hobbit Treehouse. The completed treehouse is shown on the cover. See simple building instructions on page 88.

For Your Inspiration

Many of the treehouses and play-houses in these photos were built by our readers who had little or no building experience. They did not hire expensive builders nor spend a lot of money. What they all shared was a vision to build an exciting play structure for their kids. We think they succeeded. Please use these photographs as inspiration to build your own unique treehouse or playhouse.

Hide-Away in the Woods

Amy Kemper, who had no previous building experience, built this amazing split-level treehouse single-handedly. Nestled in a Montana forest and built over a running stream, it stands 18 feet off the ground and is heated by a wood-burning stove.

Easy-Access Treehouse

John Schroeder and his boys built this tree-house using two 4x4 posts and two trees for supports. The double-pitched roof provides shade while open sides allow for breeze and light. The treehouse can be accessed by stairs and a rope ladder for emergency escapes!
Photo by Angi McGrath.

Log Cabin in the Trees

Gerald Converse built this log treehouse on his mountain property in southern Colorado for his grandchildren, Sam and Ella. It matches his log mountain home, from the red-metal roof and log railing to the skylights. A tree grows right through the deck, helping to provide shade.

"Robinson Crusoe" Treehouse

We designed and built this treehouse based on the Robinson Crusoe tale in which a shelter was built in the trees using materials salvaged from a shipwreck. Heavy lag screws secure it to the tree, but they are disguised by adding wooden pegs.

For the structural frame, we used cedar logs and pressure-treated mini-ties. We covered the roof with bamboo and grass mats from a garden supply store. The crow's nest is made from an old whiskey barrel, and the ladder and rail are made from cedar branches. Our clients hosted a surprise party for their grandchildren to unveil the treehouse including a treasure map and a hunt for hidden treasure.

Fort Knox in Quebec

David Knox and his son built this 12-foot-high treehouse in Quebec. They shingled it with cedar shakes. The skylight is made out of Plexiglas and sealed with latex caulking.

Fun Summer House

This treehouse was a great summer project for the Nordlund family, who built it in about 90 hours (with kids helping!). They used tongue and groove siding that was salvaged from a neighbor's remodeled house and installed a 4x4 skylight and four windows—all "boneyard" finds.

Poplar Hobbit House

Ken Patty, an engineer in a rural area of Georgia, saw the Hobbit Treehouse on our Web site and designed and built this very unique version of the project for his 8-year-old son. He built in a 2-foot-diameter Poplar tree, using the treehouse design for a single tree and building about 8 feet from the ground. The clapboard siding is stained green to blend in with the forest. The treehouse has a curved roof and a hand-crafted door with a stained-glass window.

Devin's Station

This treehouse, named "Devin's Station" was built entirely by 5-year-old Devin and his dad, Burt, who live in Louisiana. They used a lot of pulleys and cleats, and built the treehouse in one tree with a ladder leading to a trap door in the floor. The play hut has screened windows, helping to make the space perfect for camping out. A mailbox on the tree holds important messages.

Morris
Forest Fantasy

Dave Morris built this log treehouse in Idaho for his four kids. It features a front door decorated with rope and a hatchet handle. Morris built the treehouse of 4x4s rounded on one side only, so the logs fit flat together and don't need caulk. He sprays it once a year with a good wood sealer. He built an all-wood ladder, with dowels for rungs. Most of the lumber was given to him from construction sites, saving them hauling fees and saving him an estimated $6,000. Inside, rope bunk beds fold up against the walls.

Because the treehouse is only in one tree, there is very little tree movement in the roof. Between the roof and the tree, Morris left a 5-inch space and used tarpaper.

Today Show Treeless Treehouse

NBC television contacted us to build a "treehouse" on the *Today Show* with Matt Lauer and Katie Couric. Since there are no suitable trees near the NBC studios, we decided to build this triangular-shaped "treeless treehouse" in Rockefeller Plaza. We pre-built the structure at home, making sure everything fit perfectly, disassembled it and then transported it to New York City. Our daughter, niece and some neighborhood kids helped reassemble the treehouse during the show.

Family Fortress

For the Suttins, building this treehouse was a fun and rewarding family experience, with everyone pitching in. In the true spirit of traditional treehouse building, they used salvaged lumber to construct a sturdy platform and a snug little house, allowing the tree to enter and exit at will.

Elegant Stump Gazebo Steven Hinshaw built this "family" treehouse on top of a 500-year-old Sitka Spruce stump. A stream runs right through the base. Steven built the gazebo with a kit from JR WoodCraft (see *Resources*). He designed and built the supporting structure and walkway made of locally milled yellow cedar and recycled beams from a house he helped tear down. The gazebo offers a cozy place to relax or roast marshmallows in the deck fireplace.

Snow-Laced Hobbit Retreat

We built this Hobbit Treehouse for the Patricof's grand-children, Lily and Nina, in Eastern Long Island. Snowfall on the intricate rope railing creates the illusion of white lace, adding grace to a winter day. (See step-by-step building instructions beginning on page 88.)

Diamond in the Rough

The Mayer family built this beautiful treehouse in Alberta, Canada. Although their kids are now grown, this gem still stands proud in the woods.

Romanian Safe House

Nadine Piclisan-Perrin and her husband built this fabulous playhouse/treehouse in Romania where they run a day-care center and residence for girls who used to live on the street.

Stairs to the Sky

Dan and Annette Nowosielski built this treehouse for their son and daughter. After completing the decks, they built the treehouse on the ground in sections and used a lawn tractor and pulley system to lift them 25 feet up to the deck. Access to the treehouse is by means of a ladder that can be pivoted up like a drawbridge to prevent little children from climbing up unsupervised.

Anderson Playhouse

Carol and Dave Anderson built this playhouse for their two kids. The walls are made from old power poles (Dave is a line man) cut into 6-inch wide pieces, cemented in place with wet mortar. It has a loft area with a bed and lookout window (see photo of playhouse interior on the back cover).

English Playhouse with Porch

This 8x10 playhouse was the first building project for Richard Gibbs. It took him 8 full days to complete. He added electric cable to provide light and music.

Child's Play

This traditional playhouse provided hours of privacy and a perfect place for imaginative games for Nikki and Alex Bergsma when they were younger.

Owl Patrol

Moving up to a treehouse, Alex and Nikki share this four-post fort with a resident owl who flies overhead, patrolling the deck daily. They use the treehouse for sleepovers and hide-and-seek adventures.

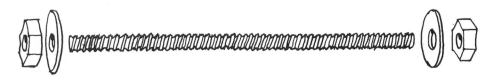

Threaded Rods

Professional tree experts often use threaded rods in cases where wire cabling is not practical *(see Figure 10)*. This is a good solution to hold beams together when building treehouses Threaded rods are much cheaper than bolts and can be cut (using a hack saw) to any desired length. Once cut, you may need to file off the burr left at the end of the rod so that the nut will screw on.

When bolting to a tree don't use anything less thick than a $1/2$-inch-diameter rod. In heavier treehouses, use $5/8$- or $3/4$-inch-diameter rods.

Never girdle a tree or cut a ring completely around the trunk. A hole made in a healthy tree should heal in one season.

> **Tip:**
>
> Use long auger bits (with an extension bit if necessary) to make the holes. This is much easier than using flat spade bits.

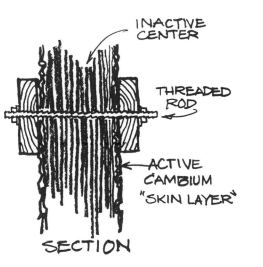

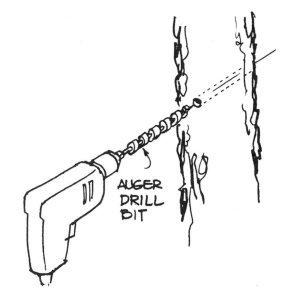

Figure 10: Threaded Rod

Flexible Connections

Because trees move with the wind, flexible connections may be necessary, especially as you build higher up in a tree. The following illustrations on pages 49–51 show several different situations you may encounter and solutions for them.

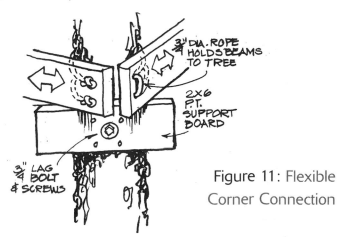

Figure 11: Flexible Corner Connection

Flexible Connections

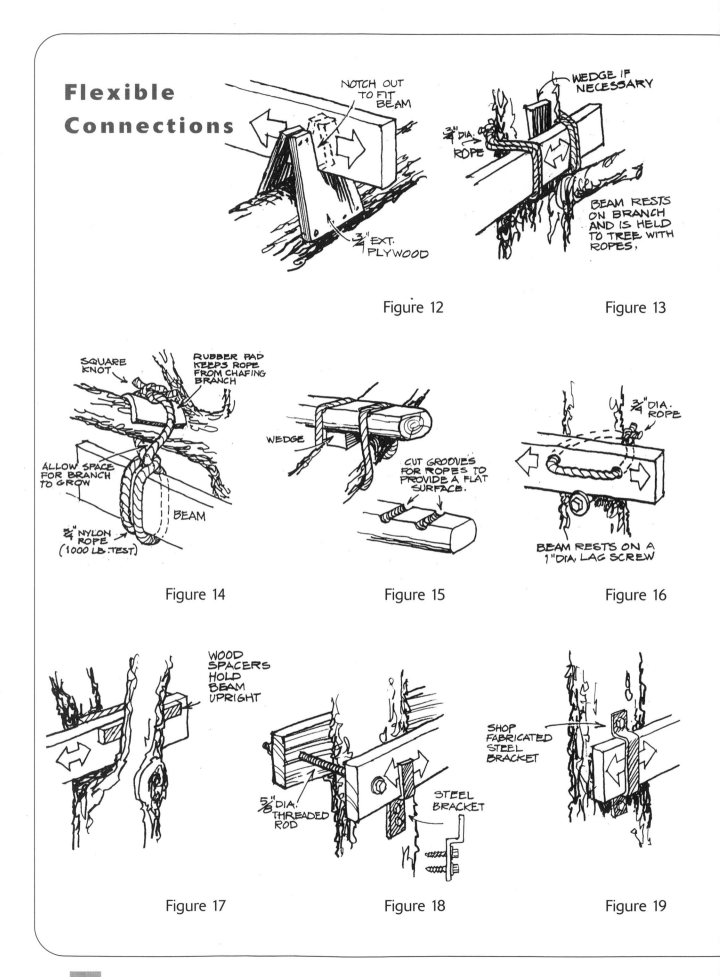

NOTCH OUT TO FIT BEAM

¾" EXT. PLYWOOD

Figure 12

WEDGE IF NECESSARY

¾" DIA. ROPE

BEAM RESTS ON BRANCH AND IS HELD TO TREE WITH ROPES.

Figure 13

SQUARE KNOT

RUBBER PAD KEEPS ROPE FROM CHAFING BRANCH

ALLOW SPACE FOR BRANCH TO GROW

BEAM

¾" NYLON ROPE (1000 LB. TEST)

Figure 14

WEDGE

CUT GROOVES FOR ROPES TO PROVIDE A FLAT SURFACE.

Figure 15

¾" DIA. ROPE

BEAM RESTS ON A 1" DIA. LAG SCREW

Figure 16

WOOD SPACERS HOLD BEAM UPRIGHT

Figure 17

⅝" DIA. THREADED ROD

STEEL BRACKET

Figure 18

SHOP FABRICATED STEEL BRACKET

Figure 19

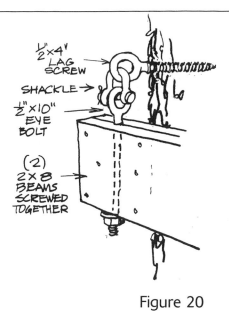

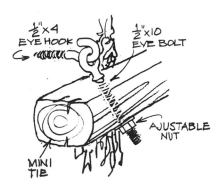

Figure 20

Figure 21

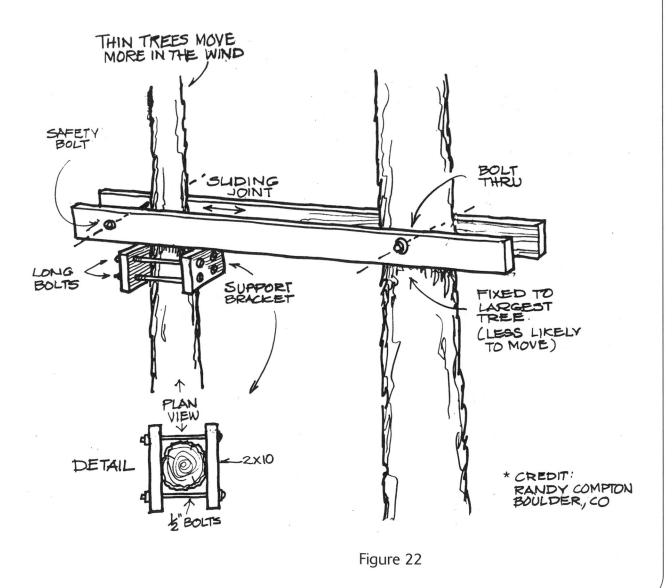

THIN TREES MOVE MORE IN THE WIND

SAFETY BOLT

SLIDING JOINT

BOLT THRU

LONG BOLTS

SUPPORT BRACKET

FIXED TO LARGEST TREE (LESS LIKELY TO MOVE)

PLAN VIEW

DETAIL

2X10

½" BOLTS

* CREDIT: RANDY COMPTON BOULDER, CO

Figure 22

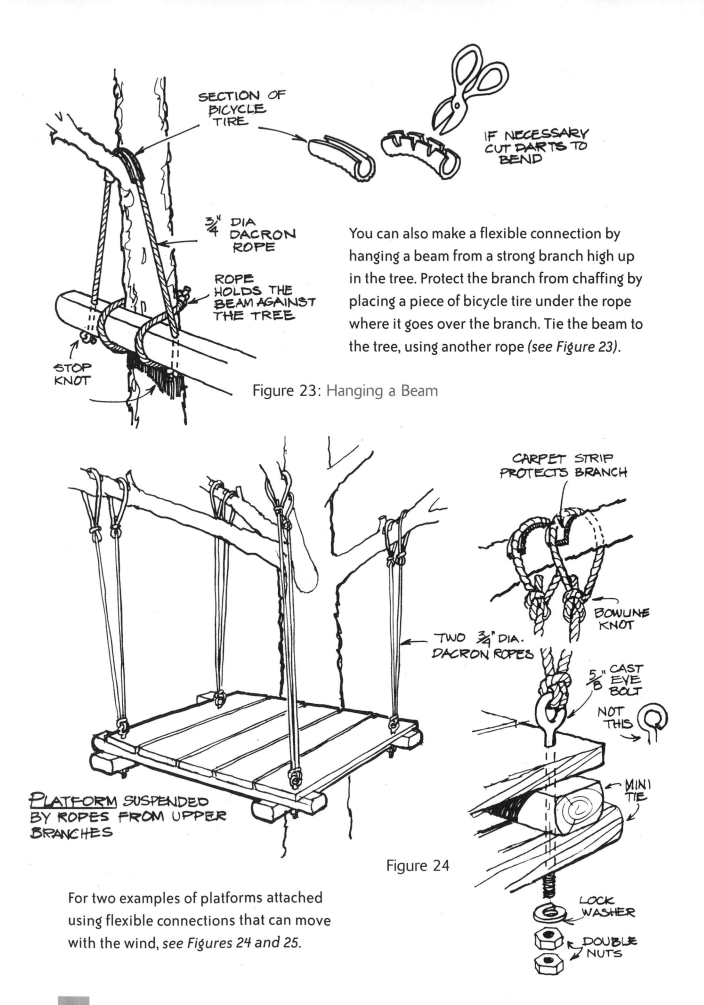

SECTION OF BICYCLE TIRE

IF NECESSARY CUT DARTS TO BEND

3/4" DIA DACRON ROPE

ROPE HOLDS THE BEAM AGAINST THE TREE

STOP KNOT

You can also make a flexible connection by hanging a beam from a strong branch high up in the tree. Protect the branch from chaffing by placing a piece of bicycle tire under the rope where it goes over the branch. Tie the beam to the tree, using another rope (*see Figure 23*).

Figure 23: Hanging a Beam

CARPET STRIP PROTECTS BRANCH

TWO 3/4" DIA. DACRON ROPES

BOWLINE KNOT

5/8" CAST EYE BOLT

NOT THIS

MINI TIE

PLATFORM SUSPENDED BY ROPES FROM UPPER BRANCHES

Figure 24

LOCK WASHER

DOUBLE NUTS

For two examples of platforms attached using flexible connections that can move with the wind, *see Figures 24 and 25.*

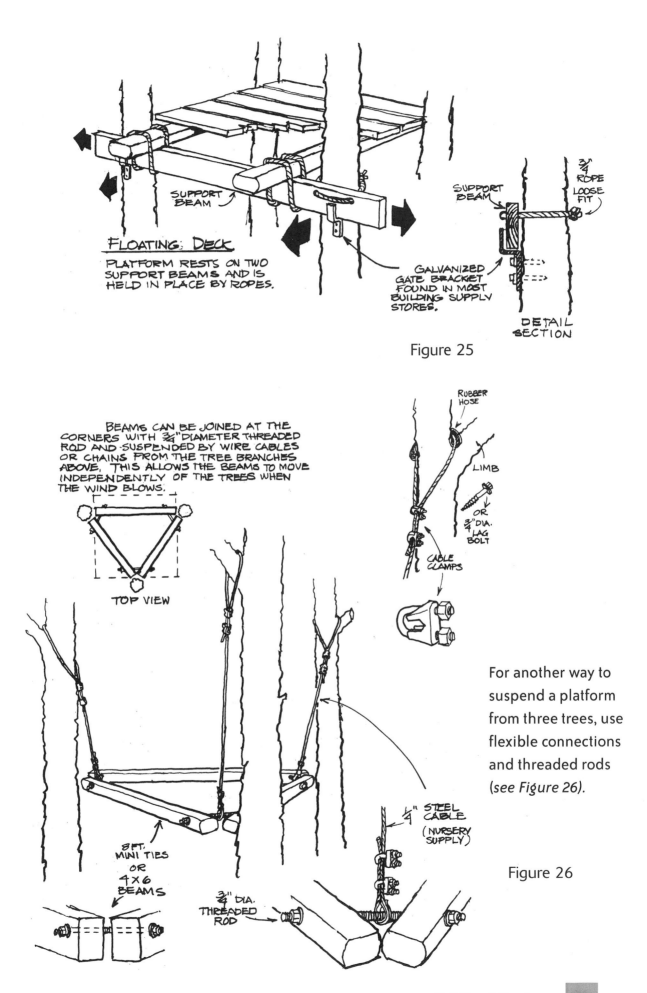

FLOATING DECK

PLATFORM RESTS ON TWO
SUPPORT BEAMS AND IS
HELD IN PLACE BY ROPES.

SUPPORT
BEAM

SUPPORT
BEAM

3/4" ROPE
LOOSE FIT

GALVANIZED
GATE BRACKET
FOUND IN MOST
BUILDING SUPPLY
STORES.

DETAIL
SECTION

Figure 25

BEAMS CAN BE JOINED AT THE
CORNERS WITH 3/4" DIAMETER THREADED
ROD AND SUSPENDED BY WIRE CABLES
OR CHAINS FROM THE TREE BRANCHES
ABOVE. THIS ALLOWS THE BEAMS TO MOVE
INDEPENDENTLY OF THE TREES WHEN
THE WIND BLOWS.

TOP VIEW

RUBBER
HOSE

LIMB

OR
3/4" DIA.
LAG
BOLT

CABLE
CLAMPS

For another way to
suspend a platform
from three trees, use
flexible connections
and threaded rods
(see Figure 26).

Figure 26

8 FT.
MINI TIES
OR
4 X 6
BEAMS

3/4" DIA.
THREADED
ROD

1/4" STEEL
CABLE
(NURSERY
SUPPLY)

Rope

Don't be afraid to use rope when building your treehouse. Shipbuilders and sailors have relied on ropes for centuries to support tremendous loads in gale-force winds. Today's synthetic ropes are almost twice as strong as the manila ropes that were used in the past and should last a decade before fraying or rotting. The one exception is Polypropylene rope that deteriorates in sunlight and forms abrasive whiskers on its surface. We recommend Dacron rope for most situations; however, nylon rope is best where a certain amount of stretch is necessary.

According to Defender Marine Supply (*see Resources*), 3/4-inch-diameter Dacron rope has a breaking strength of 11,000 pounds or about 5 tons. An average size 6x7-foot treehouse may only weigh about 1,500 pounds. Even taking into consideration that knots like a square knot or a rolling hitch can weaken the rope by 50 percent, there should still be ample leeway. In addition, the rope strength should be even stronger, because you will most likely be using four ropes, not one, to suspend your treehouse. The advantage of rope is that it can be used to make flexible connections, allowing the treehouse to flex in the wind.

Cutting Rope

To cut rope, tightly wrap tape around the rope and use a chisel to cut it in half, hitting it sharply with one blow (*see Figure 27*).

Rope Whipping

To keep the ends of rope from unraveling, lay an open-ended loop of marlin line (waxed cord) along the end of the rope. Next, tightly wind the line around the rope towards the loop (away from the end). When the turns become as wide as the diameter of rope, cut the line and poke it through the end of the loop. Pull the other end of the line and the loop will disappear under the windings. Cut off the loose ends (*see Figure 28*).

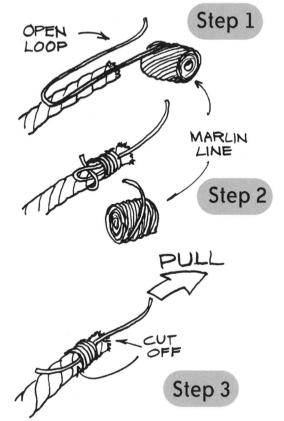

Figure 28

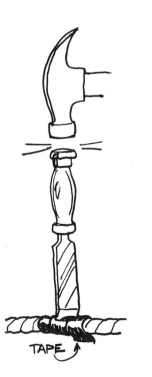

Figure 27

Sealing

To seal the ends of a nylon or Dacron rope, heat them with a propane torch or match and "paddle" the end with a putty knife while the end is melting *(see Figure 29)*.

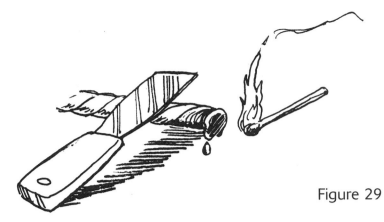

Figure 29

Knots to Know

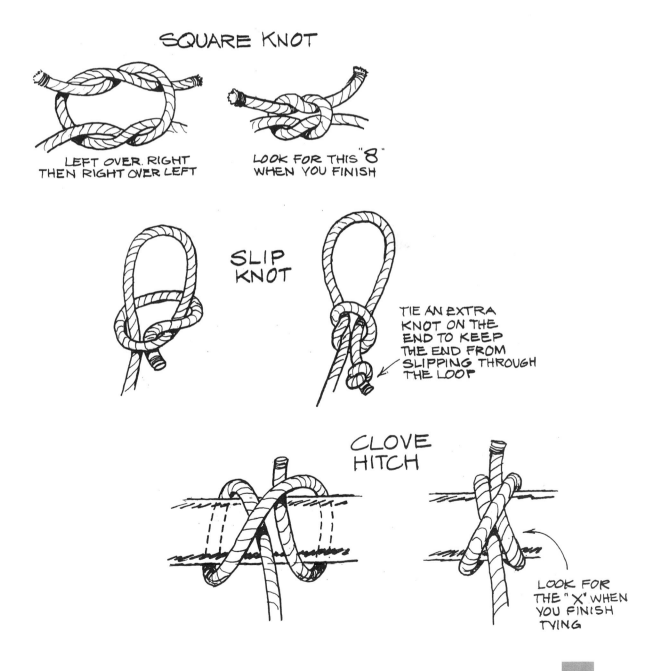

SQUARE KNOT

LEFT OVER RIGHT THEN RIGHT OVER LEFT

LOOK FOR THIS "8" WHEN YOU FINISH

SLIP KNOT

TIE AN EXTRA KNOT ON THE END TO KEEP THE END FROM SLIPPING THROUGH THE LOOP

CLOVE HITCH

LOOK FOR THE "X" WHEN YOU FINISH TYING

Knots to Know

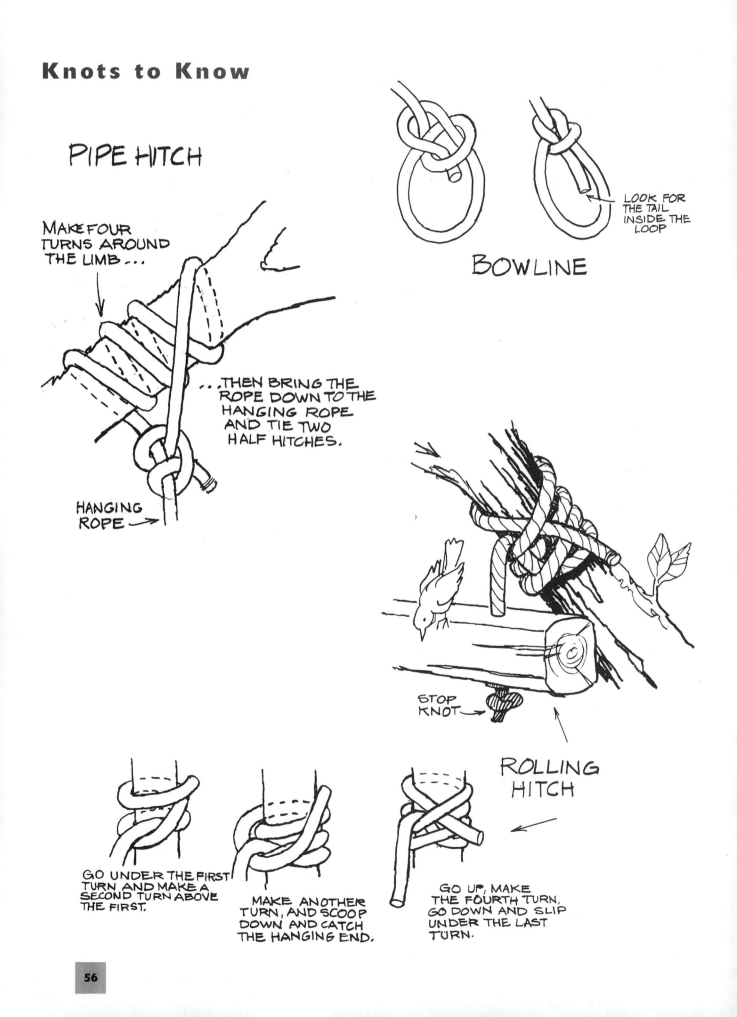

PIPE HITCH

MAKE FOUR TURNS AROUND THE LIMB...

...THEN BRING THE ROPE DOWN TO THE HANGING ROPE AND TIE TWO HALF HITCHES.

HANGING ROPE →

BOWLINE

LOOK FOR THE TAIL INSIDE THE LOOP

STOP KNOT →

ROLLING HITCH

GO UNDER THE FIRST TURN AND MAKE A SECOND TURN ABOVE THE FIRST.

MAKE ANOTHER TURN, AND SCOOP DOWN AND CATCH THE HANGING END.

GO UP, MAKE THE FOURTH TURN, GO DOWN AND SLIP UNDER THE LAST TURN.

SHACKLE

LAP LINK

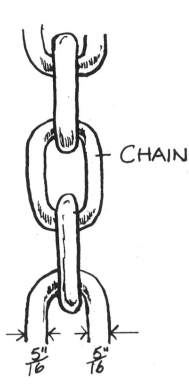
CHAIN

5"/16   5"/16

Chain

Chain is sometimes used to suspend large treehouses or to support flexible bridges between treehouses, however, it is more often used in public playground equipment where vandalism is an issue. Chain is difficult to cut and requires a vise to clamp it while it is sawed with a hack saw or a reciprocating saw. Lengths of chain are fastened together with shackles or metal lap links.

Surprisingly, chain is not as strong as rope, yet it is three times more expensive. For example, $5/16$-inch chain (actually $5/8$ inch when you add the other side of the link) has a working load of only 1,900 pounds, whereas $5/8$-inch Dacron rope has a breaking strength of 8,910 pounds, more than four times the strength of chain.

Wire Rope

Stainless steel wire rope, used in sailboat rigging, can withstand tremendous loads, is much stronger than chain (per pound), and does not rust. The breaking strength of a $3/16$-inch wire rope is 4,000 pounds (two tons). The rope costs about $1.50 per foot. If you use wire rope, make sure to buy some inexpensive $20 cable cutters (that can cut wire rope up to $3/16$ inch thick) since bolt cutters or tin snips won't cut it. Wire rope and cable cutters can be purchased at any marine supply store or ordered from a marine catalog (see Resources). Wire rope is joined together using oval or round copper sleeves that are compressed with a special swaging tool.

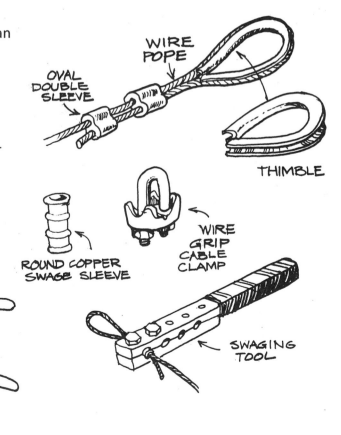

WIRE ROPE

OVAL DOUBLE SLEEVE

THIMBLE

ROUND COPPER SWAGE SLEEVE

WIRE GRIP CABLE CLAMP

CABLE CUTTER $3/16$" MAX.

SWAGING TOOL

Cables

Tree cables are thicker and heavier than wire rope. Arborists use them to repair trees that have been damaged by the wind and weather. Tree cables are joined using cable clamps (sometimes called wire grips) that are readily available at most hardware stores. Make sure you buy the correct size for the cable you use. Both cables and wire rope require thimbles when they are joined to eyebolts or turnbuckles in order to distribute the load evenly. Another way to attach tree cables is to use wire "tree grips" sold at most landscape supply centers *(see Resources)*.

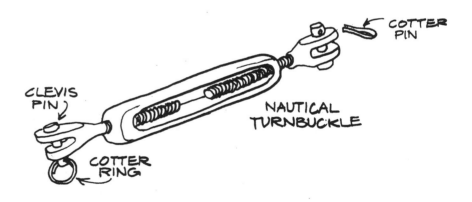

THIMBLE

GALVANIZED CABLE

TREE GRIP USED WITH LANDSCAPING CABLE

¼" BREAKING STRENGTH 3,150 LBS.

Turnbuckles

The slack or tension in wire rope or cables may need to be adjusted and turnbuckles were invented for this purpose. Most hardware stores sell an inexpensive type of turnbuckle that can be adjusted to take up the slack in the cable by 3 to 4 inches.

COTTER PIN

CLEVIS PIN

NAUTICAL TURNBUCKLE

COTTER RING

Beams

The first job in building a treehouse is to get two heavy beams securely fastened and level with each other in the tree or trees. To do this you may need to add a post to make up for a missing tree. Keep in mind that the trees or posts do not have to be perfectly square with each other to support the floor frame. This is the foundation to your house and should be a strong as possible if it is to last.

Beams/Planning

Step 1

To determine where the first beam goes, use duct tape to attach a level to a 1x2 board 10 feet long. Place this piece of wood on branches where the beam will go and mark points of contact with duct tape.

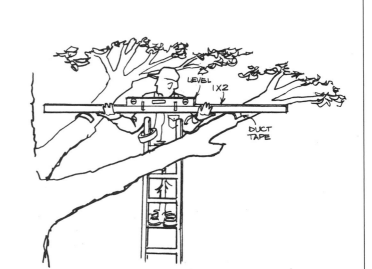

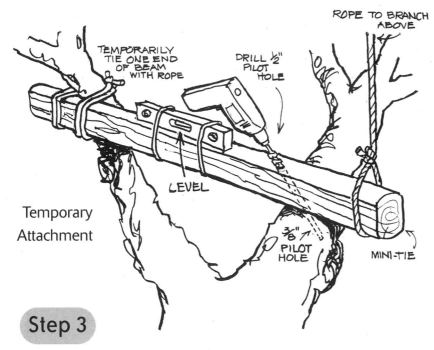

Temporary Attachment

Step 2

Use rope to temporarily attach one end of beam to tree.

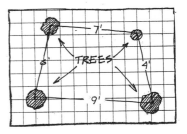

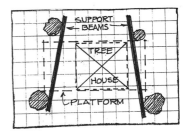

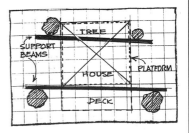

Step 3

If you build in several trees, plan where to place your first two support beams by making a sketch like this to show the distance between the trees. Photocopy your sketch and draw as many different ways you can think of to place your support beams in the trees. Draw in the platform and make a dotted line where the treehouse would be located on the platform. Remember neither the platform nor the treehouse have to be rectangular, however, it will be easier to construct if they are.

Attaching Beams

Step 1

The first piece of lumber that you attach to the tree is the most important. It MUST BE LEVEL and should be strong enough to support the entire weight of the treehouse plus its occupants (and maybe even an overweight building inspector!). Most likely, use 2x8s for treehouse beams that span 10 to 12 feet between trees and 2x10s that span 12 to 14 feet.

Step 2

Hold a level on top of the beam. Lift the other end of the beam up until it is level and hold it in place with a rope tied to a branch above.

Step 3

Drill a $1/2$-inch-diameter hole through the beam and a $3/8$-inch pilot hole into the tree (to hold the lag screw).

Step 4

Using a $1/2$-inch socket wrench, screw the $1/2$-inch-diameter lag screw into the beam and tree. Attach the other end the same way.

Tip:
One-half inch is the minimum diameter lag screw to use when attaching beams.

Braces

Quite often you will need to support a beam with a diagonal (knee) brace. The best way to accomplish this is to build it on the ground and hoist it up into the tree. Use a rope attached to a pulley on a branch higher up in the tree. Find the best position for the beam and hold it there with another rope while you screw it to the tree. Always use $1/2$-inch-diameter lag screws (bolts) or larger. Bolts that are $3/8$ inch in diameter have been known to break off.

You may find that you have to shim out the bottom of the brace with a small piece of wood to make it line up plumb with the beam. This means that the bottom lag screw will have to be longer. Make sure the beam is level before attaching it to the tree. The beam and brace do not have to be pressure-treated wood.

Often the first beam is the hardest to install in a tree. Using the method given here makes it easier to level the beam and allows for some movement in the tree limbs. It also makes it easier to remove the treehouse if it has to come down at a later date. The two lag screw holes will not injure a healthy tree.

If you only have one tree to build in, with branches too high to reach, attach a strong beam to the tree, using knee braces for support. Use two 4x4 posts to support a level platform attached to the beam and the post. For other solutions for building in one tree, *see illustrations on pages 61–63.*

For building a treehouse on a stump, see Steve Hinshaw's Gazebo built on stump in Photo Section 2 and illustrations on page 64.

For attaching the first beams when you are building a treehouse in two trees, *see illustrations on page 65.*

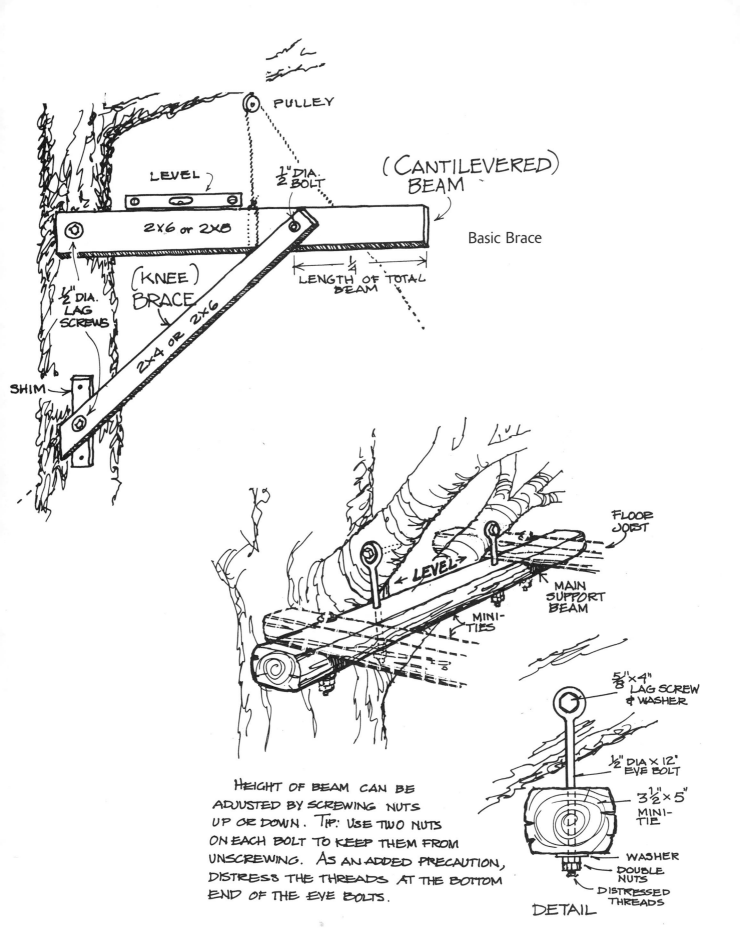

PULLEY

LEVEL

1/2" DIA. BOLT

(CANTILEVERED) BEAM

Basic Brace

2X6 or 2X8

(KNEE) BRACE

1/2" DIA. LAG SCREWS

2X4 OR 2X6

SHIM

LENGTH OF TOTAL BEAM

1/4

FLOOR JOIST

LEVEL

MAIN SUPPORT BEAM

MINI-TIES

5/8" × 4" LAG SCREW & WASHER

1/2" DIA × 12" EYE BOLT

3 1/2" × 5" MINI-TIE

WASHER

DOUBLE NUTS

DISTRESSED THREADS

DETAIL

HEIGHT OF BEAM CAN BE ADJUSTED BY SCREWING NUTS UP OR DOWN. TIP: USE TWO NUTS ON EACH BOLT TO KEEP THEM FROM UNSCREWING. AS AN ADDED PRECAUTION, DISTRESS THE THREADS AT THE BOTTOM END OF THE EYE BOLTS.

Leveling First Brace

Braces

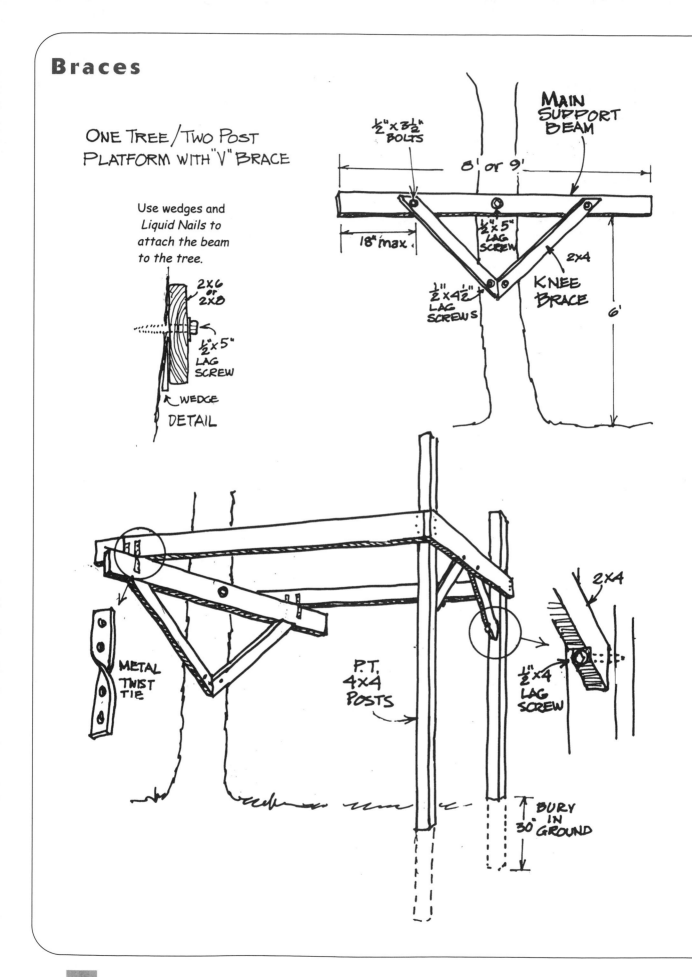

ONE TREE/TWO POST
PLATFORM WITH "V" BRACE

Use wedges and
Liquid Nails to
attach the beam
to the tree.

2×6
or
2×8

½"×5"
LAG
SCREW

WEDGE

DETAIL

½"×3½"
BOLTS

MAIN
SUPPORT
BEAM

8' or 9'

18" max.

½"×5"
LAG
SCREW

2×4

KNEE
BRACE

½"×4½"
LAG
SCREWS

6'

METAL
TWIST
TIE

P.T.
4×4
POSTS

2×4

½"×4
LAG
SCREW

BURY
IN
30" GROUND

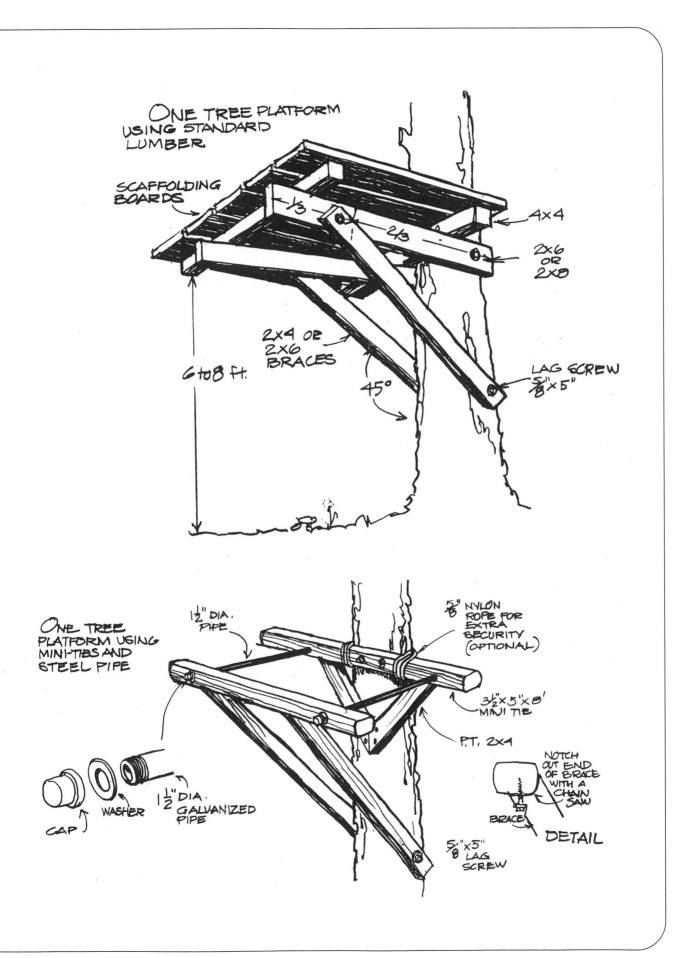

ONE TREE PLATFORM
USING STANDARD
LUMBER

SCAFFOLDING
BOARDS

1/3

2/3

4×4

2×6
OR
2×8

2×4 OR
2×6
BRACES

6 to 8 ft.

45°

LAG SCREW
5/8"×5"

ONE TREE
PLATFORM USING
MINI-TIES AND
STEEL PIPE

1 1/2" DIA.
PIPE

5/8" NYLON
ROPE FOR
EXTRA
SECURITY
(OPTIONAL)

3 1/2"×5"×8'
MINI TIE

P.T. 2×4

CAP

WASHER

1 1/2" DIA.
GALVANIZED
PIPE

5/8"×5"
LAG
SCREW

NOTCH
OUT END
OF BRACE
WITH A
CHAIN
SAW

BRACE

DETAIL

SOMETIMES A TREE MAY HAVE TO BE REMOVED FROM YOUR PROPERTY. INSTEAD OF REMOVING THE WHOLE TREE, SAVE 6 OR 7 FEET OF THE TREE BASE AND USE IT AS A FOUNDATION FOR A TREE HOUSE.

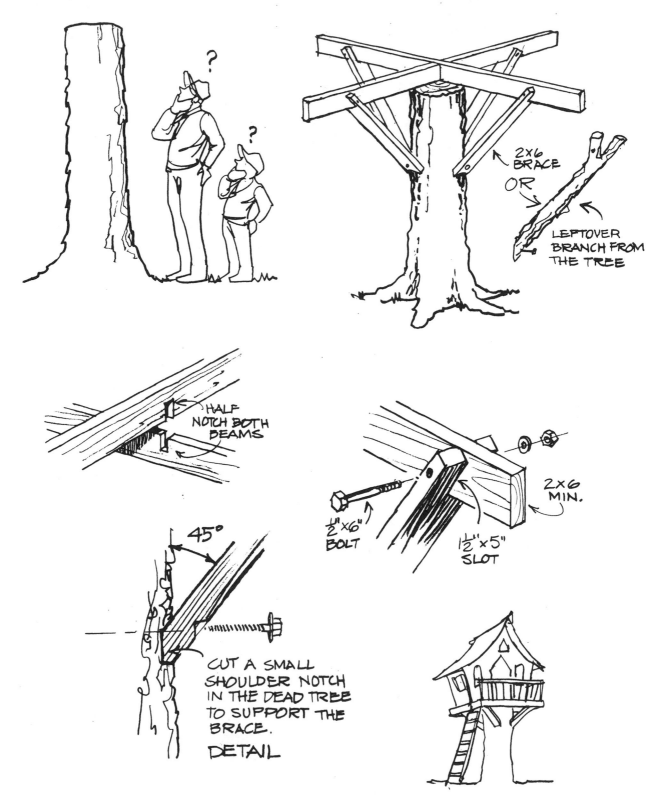

2X6 BRACE
OR
LEFTOVER BRANCH FROM THE TREE

HALF NOTCH BOTH BEAMS

2X6 MIN.

½"X6" BOLT

1½"X5" SLOT

45°

CUT A SMALL SHOULDER NOTCH IN THE DEAD TREE TO SUPPORT THE BRACE.

DETAIL

Treestump House

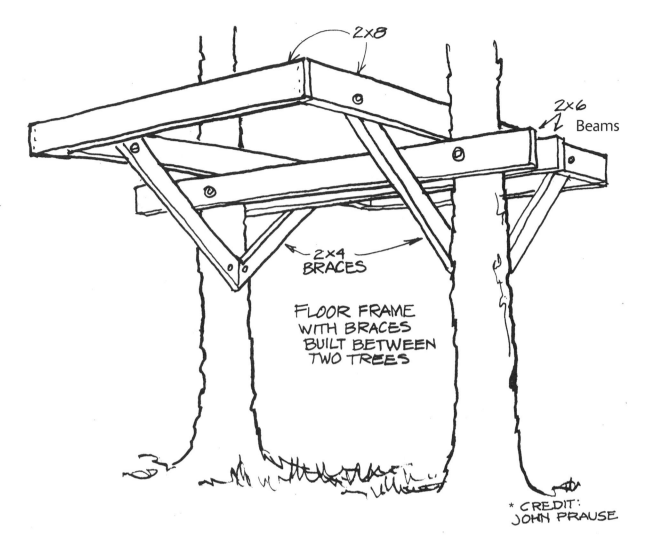

2x8

2x6

Beams

2x4
BRACES

FLOOR FRAME
WITH BRACES
BUILT BETWEEN
TWO TREES

* CREDIT:
JOHN PRAUSE

Using Two Trees

Access to the Treehouse

There are many ways to gain access to a treehouse—such as rope ladders, gangplanks, rope bridges, and stepladders, but we feel one of the best is a set of well-constructed stairs. Over the years we have observed that kids use a treehouse more if it has easy access. Stairs are also the safest way to get into a treehouse.

Building Stairs

Stairs are often the last thing considered when building a treehouse, which is a mistake. A good, solid, easy-to-climb set of stairs makes building and using the treehouse much easier (*see instructions on next page*). The stairs shown here only take a couple of hours to build and cost about $15 in materials. Using 1x4 cleats between the steps makes it easy and fast to build and ensures that the stairs will last a long time. Remember, when building a treehouse, you will probably be climbing up the stairs more than a hundred times!

Building Stairs

Step 1

Before beginning, make sure that the ground is firm and level where the bottom of the ladder is going to rest. Place 2x6 stringers up against the floor frame of the treehouse at the angle that you want your stairs and cut off the bottom of the stringer to rest flat on the ground. Do the same to the other stringer. Measure, mark and cut off the tops of the stringers to fit against the side of the treehouse frame.

FLOOR FRAME

PLUMB

1x4 SUPPORT CLEATS

2x6 STRINGER

2x6 TREADS

LEVEL

8"

RISE

16"

Step 2

To layout the steps (treads) on the stringers, first determine the height (rise) you want your steps (typically 8 inches). Measure down that distance from the top of the stringer and mark point "A." Draw a LEVEL line from point "A" to the front edge of the stringer and mark this as point "B." Measure from "B" to the top of the stringer (point "C"). Use this measurement (B to C) to mark the other steps on the front edge of the stringer.

C

8"

LEVEL

B

D

A

2x6

8"

1x4 CLEAT

2x6 STRINGER

2x6

TREAD

Step 3

Cut each tread exactly 16 inches long. Cut two 1x4 cleats at angle "D" to support each step. Nail the 1x4 cleats to the insides of the stringers in between each tread. Screw the stringer to the treads using 3-inch galvanized screws.

TOP

1/2" PEG

PLUMB LINE

FLOOR FRAME

Step 4

When you have finished, use two 1/2-inch-diameter pegs to attach the stairs (temporarily) to the treehouse, allowing you to remove when them when not in use.

2x6 STRINGER

LEVEL LINE

BOTTOM

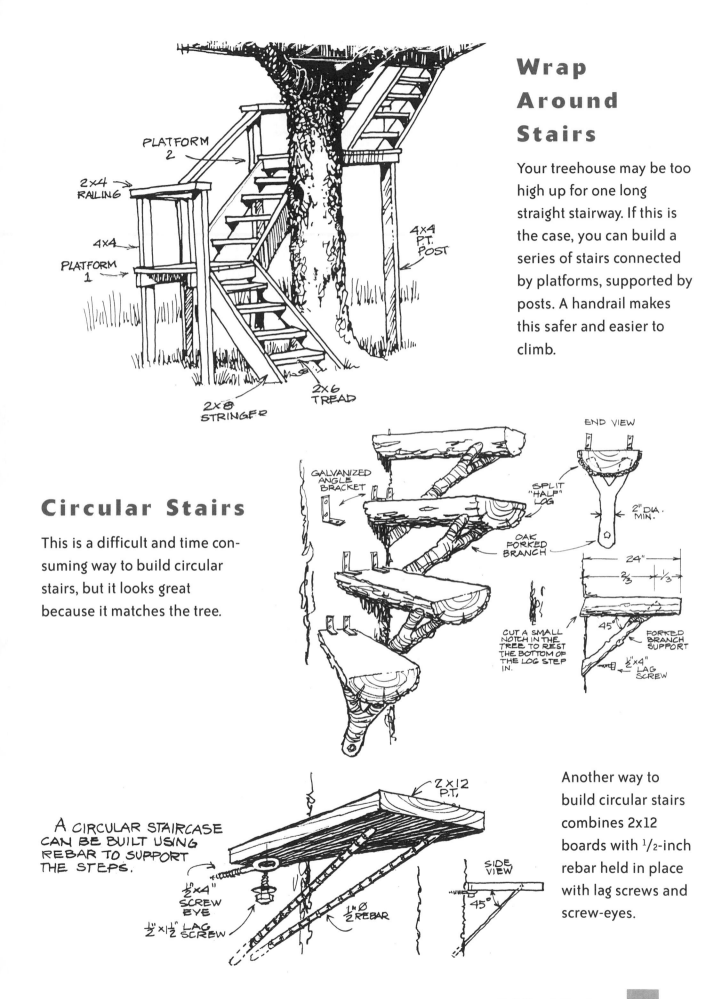

Wrap Around Stairs

Your treehouse may be too high up for one long straight stairway. If this is the case, you can build a series of stairs connected by platforms, supported by posts. A handrail makes this safer and easier to climb.

PLATFORM 2

2×4 RAILING

4×4

PLATFORM 1

2×8 STRINGER

2×6 TREAD

4×4 P.T. POST

END VIEW

GALVANIZED ANGLE BRACKET

SPLIT "HALF" LOG

2" DIA. MIN.

OAK FORKED BRANCH

24"

⅔ ⅓

45°

FORKED BRANCH SUPPORT

CUT A SMALL NOTCH IN THE TREE TO REST THE BOTTOM OF THE LOG STEP IN.

¼"×4" LAG SCREW

Circular Stairs

This is a difficult and time consuming way to build circular stairs, but it looks great because it matches the tree.

A CIRCULAR STAIRCASE CAN BE BUILT USING REBAR TO SUPPORT THE STEPS.

2×12 P.T.

½"×4" SCREW EYE

½"×1½" LAG SCREW

½"Ø REBAR

SIDE VIEW

45°

Another way to build circular stairs combines 2x12 boards with ¹/₂-inch rebar held in place with lag screws and screw-eyes.

Rope Ladder

Before building your treehouse, it's a good idea to spend some time getting to know the tree you have chosen to build in. Familiarize yourself with the branches and seek out the best opportunities for building your treehouse.

To make it easier to climb up into the tree, build a rope ladder, using ⁵/₈-inch-thick rope and 2x4 steps. To secure the ladder to the tree, tie one end of a lightweight rope to the top of the ladder and attach a heavy weight to the other end of the rope. Throw the weighted end over a high limb, directing it to fall on the ground nearby. Use this as a pulley to raise and position the ladder. Wrap the lightweight rope around the tree several times and secure it with a tight knot.

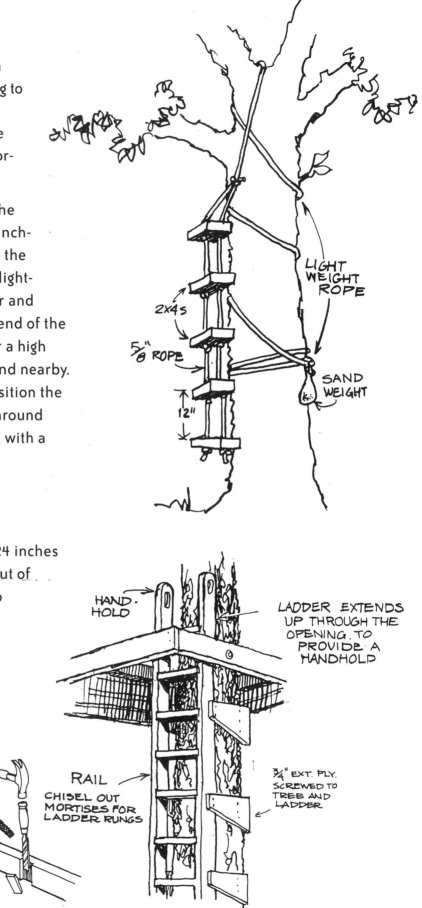

LIGHT WEIGHT ROPE

2x4s

⁵/₈" ROPE

12"

SAND WEIGHT

Permanent Ladder

For trees that are between 12 and 24 inches in diameter, cut support brackets out of ³/₄-inch-thick plywood. Cut steps to fit your tree out of 2x4s and mortise them into the two 2x4 rails. Screw the brackets to the tree and the rails on either side.

HAND-HOLD

LADDER EXTENDS UP THROUGH THE OPENING TO PROVIDE A HANDHOLD

RAIL
CHISEL OUT MORTISES FOR LADDER RUNGS

¾" EXT. PLY. SCREWED TO TREE AND LADDER

2X4 RAIL

Flexible Collar

Sometimes it is necessary to have a tree or branch pass through the roof or wall of the treehouse *(see Resources for inner tube)*.

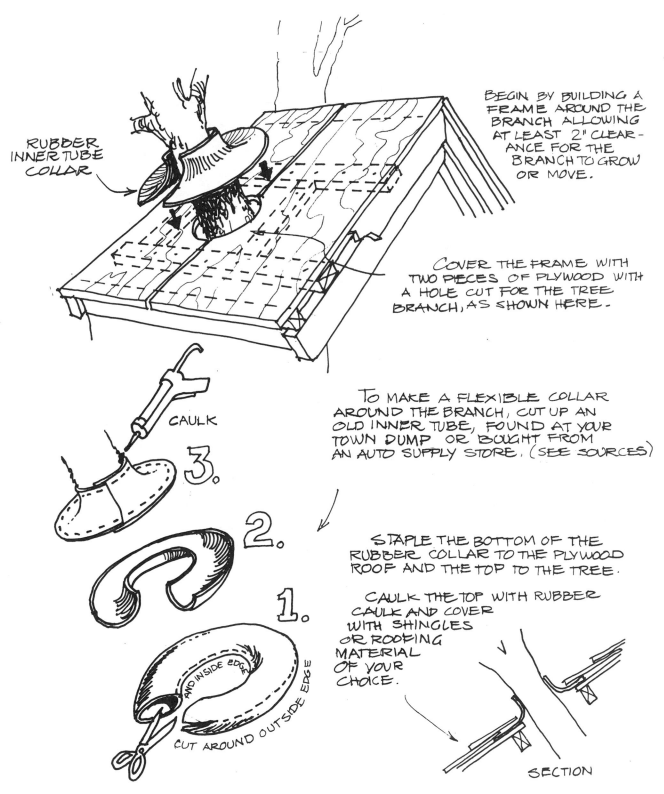

RUBBER INNER TUBE COLLAR

BEGIN BY BUILDING A FRAME AROUND THE BRANCH ALLOWING AT LEAST 2" CLEARANCE FOR THE BRANCH TO GROW OR MOVE.

COVER THE FRAME WITH TWO PIECES OF PLYWOOD WITH A HOLE CUT FOR THE TREE BRANCH, AS SHOWN HERE.

CAULK

3.

2.

1.

TO MAKE A FLEXIBLE COLLAR AROUND THE BRANCH, CUT UP AN OLD INNER TUBE, FOUND AT YOUR TOWN DUMP OR BOUGHT FROM AN AUTO SUPPLY STORE, (SEE SOURCES)

STAPLE THE BOTTOM OF THE RUBBER COLLAR TO THE PLYWOOD ROOF AND THE TOP TO THE TREE.

CAULK THE TOP WITH RUBBER CAULK AND COVER WITH SHINGLES OR ROOFING MATERIAL OF YOUR CHOICE.

AND INSIDE EDGE

CUT AROUND OUTSIDE EDGE

SECTION

THREE TREEHOUSE DESIGNS

Basic Treehouse

Someone with minimal building experience can easily build this basic treehouse in just a few weekends (*see Figures 1 and 2*). It requires only one tree and three removable bolts.

The lookout deck is great fun and allows kids to have an open view into the trees and sky. Design your own window treatment if you want it more enclosed.

✳ Materials List for the Basic Treehouse

Quantity	Description	Length	Location
(2)	3 x 5-inch mini-ties	8 feet	main support beam/braces
(6)	2x6 fir	8 feet	deck frame
(1)	2x6 fir	10 feet	deck frame
(3)	4x4 cedar posts	12 feet	posts
(10)	5/4x6 cedar decking	6 feet	decking
(6)	5/4x6 cedar decking	8 feet	decking
(2)	2x6 fir	8 feet	stair stringers
(2)	2x6 fir	10 feet	stair treads
(2)	2x4 fir	8 feet	stair rails
(4)	2x3 spruce	12 feet	wall framing
(5)	2x3 spruce	10 feet	wall framing
(5)	2x3 spruce	8 feet	wall framing
(6)	1x8 #2 pine	10 feet	side wallboards
(6)	1x8 #2 pine	12 feet	front and rear walls
(9)	1x10 #2 pine	7 feet	roof boards
(3)	1x4 #2 pine	8 feet	roof fascia boards
(2)	2x3 #2 pine	12 feet	railings
(1)	5/8 x 6-inch lag screw		center of support beam
(4)	1/2 x 6-inch lag screws		braces

fascia = vertical board nailed onto ends of rafters

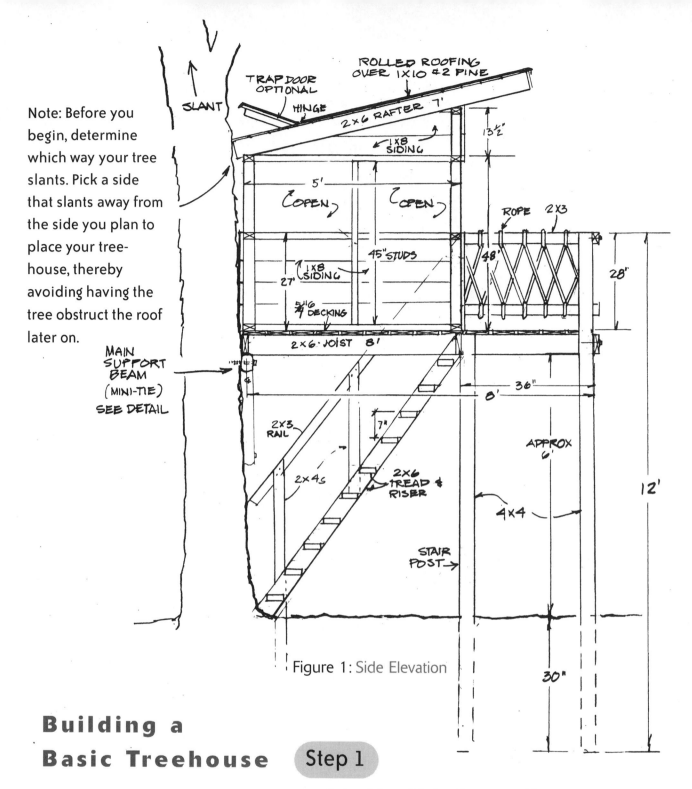

Note: Before you begin, determine which way your tree slants. Pick a side that slants away from the side you plan to place your treehouse, thereby avoiding having the tree obstruct the roof later on.

Figure 1: Side Elevation

Building a Basic Treehouse

Step 1

Attaching Main Support Beam

Drill a $5/8$-inch-diameter hole through the middle of a 7-foot-long mini-tie.

Hold the mini-tie about 6 feet off the ground against the tree and hammer a $5/8$-inch-diameter galvanized 6-inch-long lag screw and washer into the tree to make an indentation. Remove the beam and drill a $1/2$-inch-diameter hole into indentation 2 inches deep.

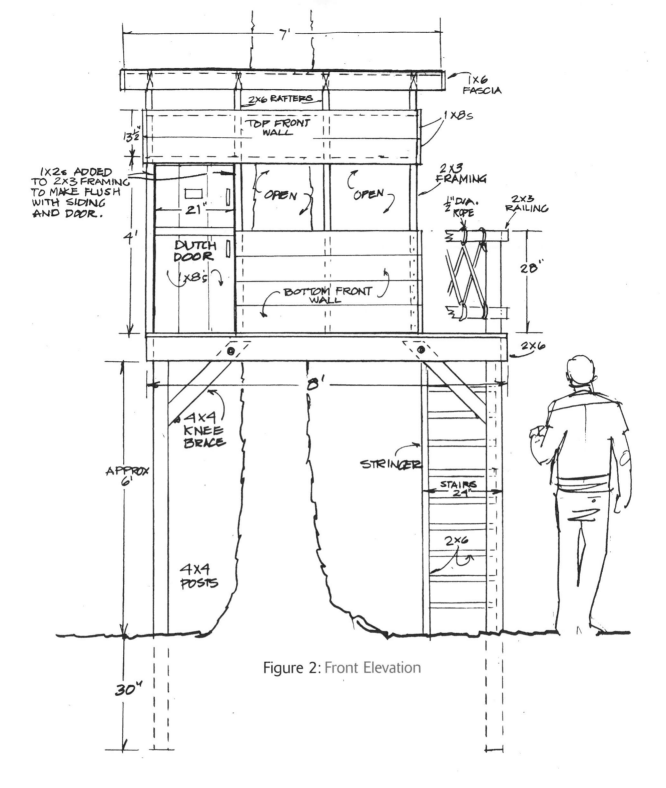

7'

1X6
FASCIA

2X6 RAFTERS

1X8s

TOP FRONT
WALL

13½"

1X2s ADDED
TO 2X3 FRAMING
TO MAKE FLUSH
WITH SIDING
AND DOOR.

OPEN

OPEN

2X3
FRAMING

½"DIA.
ROPE

2X3
RAILING

21"

4'

DUTCH
DOOR

1X8s

28"

BOTTOM FRONT
WALL

2X6

8'

4X4
KNEE
BRACE

STRINGER

APPROX
6'

STAIRS
21"

2X6

4X4
POSTS

Figure 2: Front Elevation

30"

Hold the beam up against the tree again and hammer the lag
screw through the beam and into the hole in the tree. (It is not
necessary to worry about leveling the beam at this point.)

Hammer the lag screw as hard as you can in order to catch the
threads of the lag screw in the tree, then follow the instructions
on page 48 of Building a Treehouse "Installing a Lag Screw."

(See Figures 1 and 2 for building a basic treehouse.)

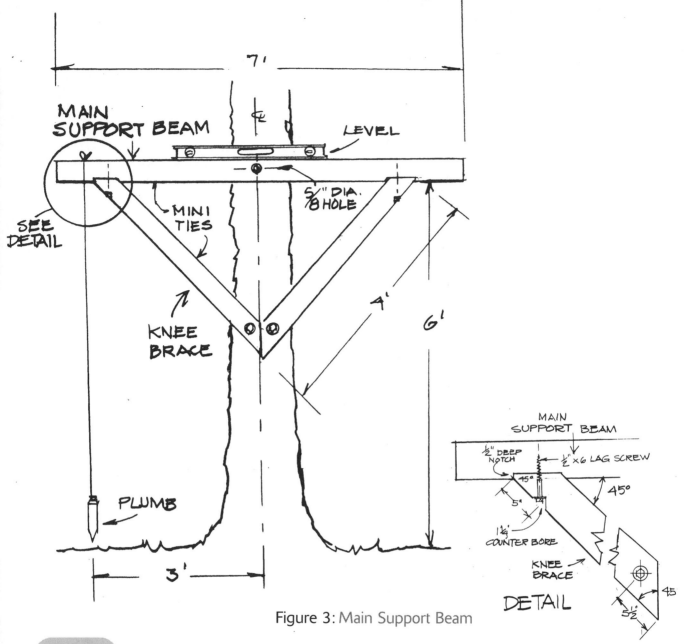

Figure 3: Main Support Beam

Setting Up Knee Braces

Place a level on top of the main support beam and tilt the beam until it is dead level. To add support to the beam, cut another mini-tie into two 4-foot pieces and make a 45-degree miter cut at each end. Mark the top ends of the two knee braces 5 inches in from the end. Use a spade drill to counter bore a $1^1/_2$-inch-diameter hole, 1 inch deep, followed by a $^1/_2$-inch-diameter hole completely through each brace. On the bottom end of the two braces, mark the face (flat) side $5^1/_2$ inches in from the end and drill a $^1/_2$-inch-diameter hole through the center of the brace, to accept a $^1/_2$-inch-diameter lag screw.

To fit the knee braces properly into the main support beam, cut a $^1/_2$-inch-deep notch in the underside of the beam. Attach the two braces to the tree and the main support beam in the same manner as before, using $5^1/_2$-inch lag screws (see Figure 3).

Step 3

Framing the Floor

Build the floor frame on level ground using six 2x6s, 8 feet long, one 2x6, 6 feet long, and one 2x6, 3 feet long. Nail two 10d 3-inch-long galvanized nails into each joint *(see Figure 4)*.

Check to make sure the frame is square and nail two temporary cross braces diagonally across to hold it in place.

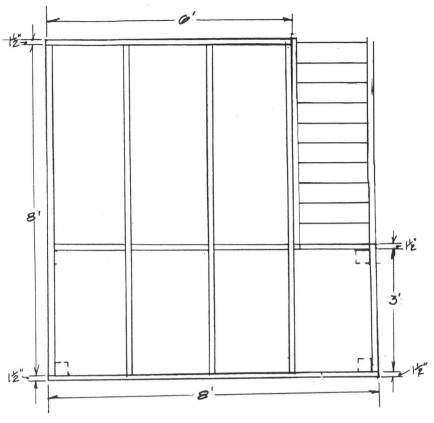

Figure 4: Floor Frame Plan

Step 4   Locating the Post Holes

To mark where the postholes should be dug, first drop a weighted string (plumb) 3 feet from the center of the main support beam and make a mark in the ground *(see Figures 3 and 5B)*.

Measure 8 feet from the mark (at a right angle to the main support beam) and place a corner stake in the ground. Measure 8 feet over from this stake (again at a right angle) and place a second stake *(see Figure 5B)*. You can check for accuracy by measuring from the second stake to the first (plumb) mark that should be 11.3 feet on the diagonal. To locate where to dig the actual postholes, measure in diagonally, at a 45-degree angle, 4 5/8 inches from each corner stake and make a mark where the center of the posts will go *(see Figure 5A)*. Follow the directions on page 29–30 for "Installing Posts."

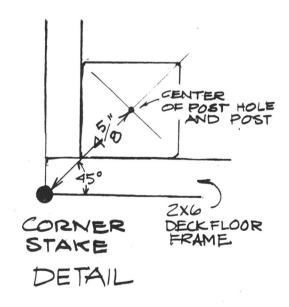

Figure 5A: Locating Post Hole

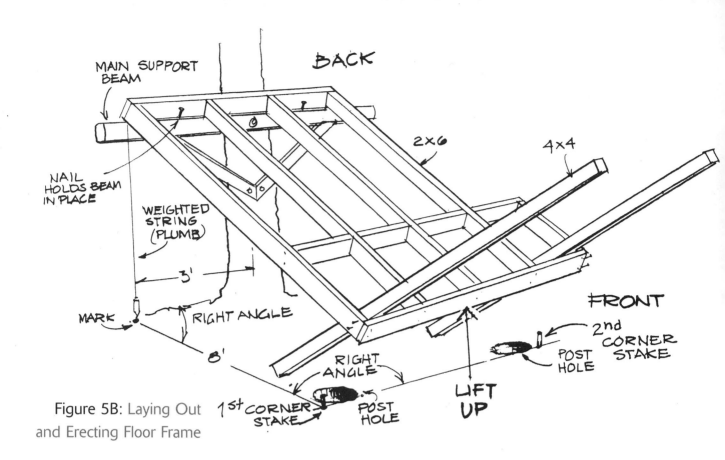

Figure 5B: Laying Out and Erecting Floor Frame

Step 5

Erecting the Floor Frame

To erect the 2x6 floor frame you need four people—two to lift the floor frame and two to slide the poles into their holes. Have a nail or screw started at each corner of the frame so when you lift the frame up you can temporarily hold it in place *(see Figure 5B)*.

Lift the back end of the frame up first and rest it on the main support beam. Then lift the front end up (with the posts inside the frame). Be careful not to let the frame slip off the main support beam. Temporarily nail or tie it in place.

Note:

Install a third post after the frame is up to help support the stairs.

Step 6　Squaring, Leveling, and Plumbing the Frame

Before you backfill the posts, check to make sure the frame is square, level, and plumb. Check for "square" by measuring the diagonals again. If it's not level, adjust it by removing the nails or screws one at a time, and resetting the frame on the posts after it is level. Finally, make sure the posts are plumb by using the level, vertically. Once the frame is square, level, and plumb, brace the posts with 1x2s and backfill the holes, as described on page 29-30, "Installing Posts."

Step 7

Attaching the Floor Frame

To permanently attach the floor frame to the main support beam, *toe-nail* (hammer at an angle) 12d, 3^1/$_2$-inch-long galvanized nails through the floor frame and into the main support beam (mini-tie).

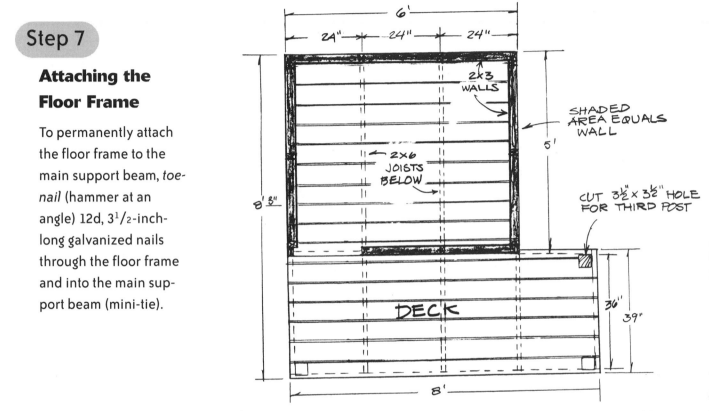

Figure 6: Plan

Step 8

Decking

Cut six pieces of ^{5}/$_4$x6 decking, 8 feet long. Cut 10 pieces of decking 6 feet long. Nail the boards to the 2x6 frame using 3-inch spiral deck nails. Since rain may come through the open windows, we recommend using open decking with ^{1}/$_2$-inch spaces between the boards, to allow the rain to drain out (*see Figures 6 and 7*).

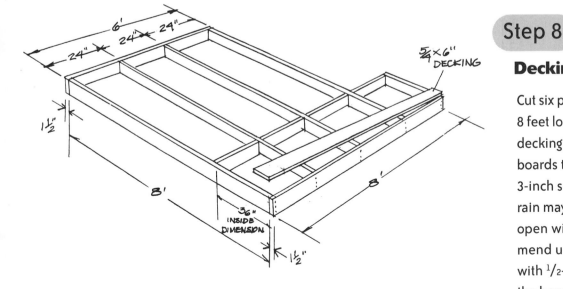

Figures 7: Deck Assembly

Step 9 — Stairs

Many people make the mistake of building the stairs last, preferring to use a ladder in the meantime. It is much easier and safer to build the stairs as soon as the deck is finished, because you will be making hundreds of trips up and down the treehouse as construction continues *(see page 66 "Building Stairs").*

You can make temporary stairs out of 2x6s and add cleats later on to add strength to the treads. Before you begin building the stairs, add the third post to help support the stairs. You will need to cut a 3¹/₂-inch-square hole in the deck for the post, using an electric jigsaw. Use 3-inch #10 galvanized screws to hold the stair treads in place.

Step 10 — Walls

Build the walls using the deck as your workspace *(see Figures 8 and 9)*. Or, if you prefer, build them on the ground and hoist them up onto the deck in dramatic fashion. This could be the making of an exciting treehouse raising party. In either case, frame the walls out of 2x3s and add the siding before standing the walls up into their final position. Have an assistant hold the wall panels up while you screw them together at the corners.

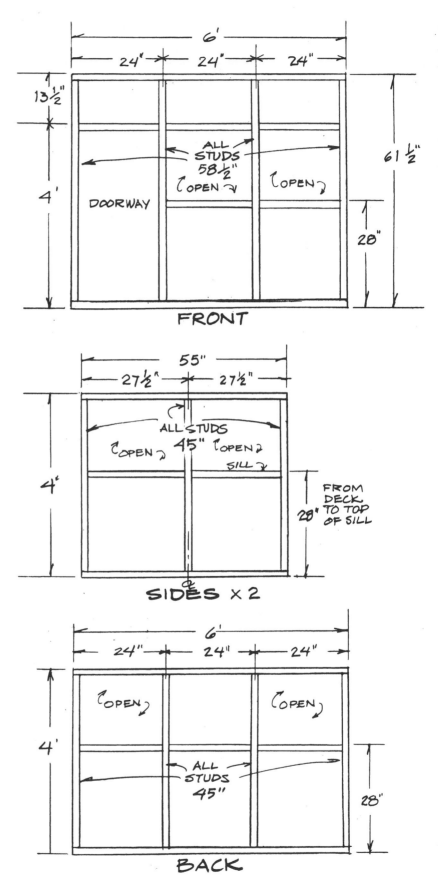

Figure 8: Wall Framing Plans

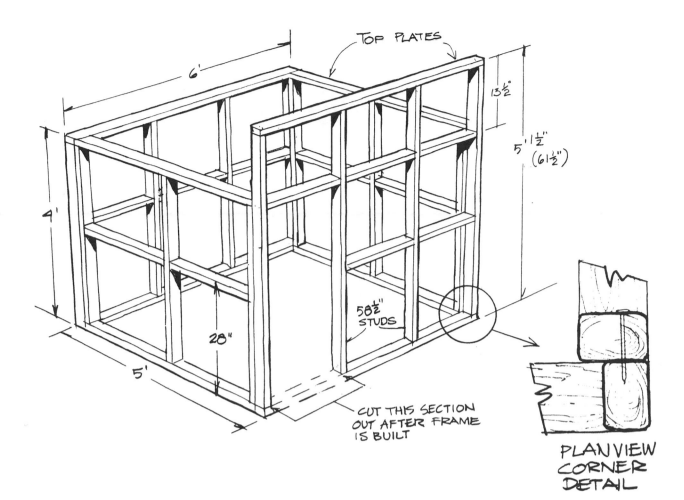

TOP PLATES

6'

13½"

5'1½"
(61½")

4'

58¼"
STUDS

28"

5'

CUT THIS SECTION
OUT AFTER FRAME
IS BUILT

PLAN VIEW
CORNER
DETAIL

Step 11

Figure 9: Wall Framing

Rafters

For the rafters, cut four 2x6s, 7 feet long *(See Figure 10)*. Before nailing them to the front and back top plates, lay one rafter on top of the plates. Mark where the rafter touches the plates and cut two notches (called "bird's mouths") in the bottom of the 2x6 to allow it to fit securely on top of the plates. Test this rafter to see if the fit is right and use it as a template to mark all the other rafters. Toenail the rafters to the top plates using 12d 3½-inch nails.

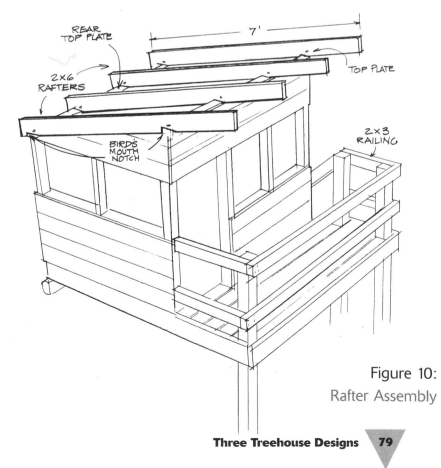

REAR
TOP PLATE

7'

2x6
RAFTERS

TOP PLATE

BIRD'S
MOUTH
NOTCH

2x3
RAILING

Figure 10:
Rafter Assembly

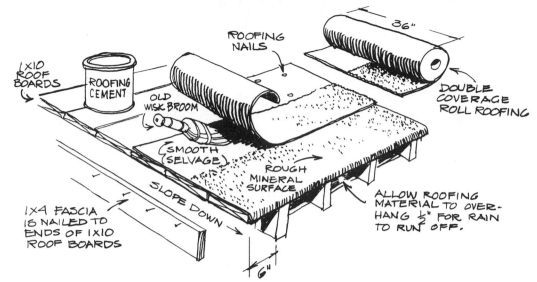

Step 12   Roof

Cover the rafters with 1x10 boards, 7 feet long, allowing them to extend over each side wall by 6 inches *(see Figures 11 and 12)*. To make the roof waterproof, cover the 1x10 roof boards with double coverage roll roofing. Since the roof of the treehouse will rarely be seen, we suggest using roll roofing as a less expensive and easier to install alternative. After you finish the roofing, nail a 1x4 fascia to the sides and the front to give the treehouse a more finished look.

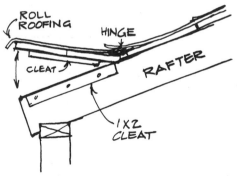

Figure 12: Optional Hatch Detail

Step 13

Rails, Door, and Hatch

Screw the 2x3 railings to the posts using 3-inch gal-vanized screws *(see Figure 10)*. Weave 1/2-inch-thick hemp rope between the railings *(see Making Rope Railings on page 31–32)*. If you are feeling adven-turesome, build a hatch in the roof for climbing up into the tree *(see Figure 12)*. The Basic Treehouse can also be built without trees *(see Figure 13)*.

Figure 13: Treeless Version

A-Frame Treehouse

The authors constructed this easy-to-build A-frame treehouse, overlooking a pond in Eastern Long Island, in 3 days using only one tree and two support posts. The awning-type windows are hinged down in inclement weather.

Fancy Lattice Playhouse

Building this playhouse was a summer project for Dave Thierry and his 5-year-old daughter. He liked the idea of having an open-air lattice house with ornate brackets and a canopy.

Maryland Meeting House

Russell Baker built this treehouse for his two daughters, Lauren and Allison. Using the building principles from one of our treehouse books and basic hand tools, he designed the hut to nestle in the curved branch of this unique tree.

Painted Playhouse

Victor Veltri built this 6x7-foot treehouse with his two kids. It is supported by one tree and three posts. The four swing-out windows were made from recycled cedar skylights and the door is half of a bi-fold closet door. Two fold-up bunk beds hang from the walls.

Rope Bridge Connecting Two Treehouses

Nick Wusz, who lives in Oregon, essentially constructed two treehouses, one to access the rope bridge and the other as the main treehouse built on one 16-inch-diameter tree. The rope bridge uses composite deck boards interlaced with polyester rope and supported by two strong cables attached to the underside of the boards.

"Pie-Rat" Ship

This photo shows a one-third-scale model of the pirate ship playhouse. When built to the dimensions shown in this book, the ship is the size of a small car—big enough for three or four small kids to play comfortably. See how-to building instructions beginning on page 96.

Sister Betsy's Poustinia

Sister Betsy discovered this hut in the forest and restored it with help from a friend. They shingled the sides and put on a new roof, slanting it so rainwater would go into the creek instead of the road. Just big enough for one person, she calls this her "prayer tree-room." In Russian the word *poustinia,* means "a place to go and look within yourself."

Pirate Tree-Fort

Susan Hellman, an occupational therapist, built this two-level treehouse for her grandchildren. It is outfitted with a ship's steering wheel, a canvas roof and a cargo net, all good for learning skills and having fun.

Stairway to the Treetops

Valerie Brouwers built this shingled treehouse on one two-trunked tree. The trunks go right through the house, extending out the roof. It was their first building project and a great success!

Treehouse-and-Tree in One

Ernesto Martinez built this tree fort for his son, Matthew, high up in one tree, allowing the spreading branches to go through the house and deck. The treehouse really becomes part of the tree. It was built using one double crossbeam across the middle and several supporting knee braces. The front deck has a rope railing and a very long ladder is used to reach the treehouse.

Three-Tree Treehouse

Colleen Parente built this study treehouse in three trees in just six weeks for her 5-year-old son. They live on a fifteen-acre parcel of land, so she found most of the materials she needed right on her property. Her only expense was for tools and rope.

Colorado Rocky Mountain High

Randy Compton and his brother built this 10x10-foot treehouse, which offers a spectacular view of the Colorado Mountains, for Randy's daughter, Meryl. The house is made from wood salvaged from an old carport. He wisely built the platform frame to be able to flex with the trees, as they bend in winds that gust as high as 70 mph. The board-and-batten siding and rough-hewn log steps enhance its rustic look.

Treehouse with Everything

Jeff and Donna Lambert surprised their kids by building this treehouse for them while they were away for a week visiting their grandparents. Together, it took them 144 hours, working from early morning until late at night. Using pressure-treated wood throughout, they built two structures connected with a bridge suspended by chains. Included in the treehouse is a slide, fire pole, cargo net, rope swing, zip line, water fountain and a basket on a pulley!

Three-Generation Two-Part Treehouse

Warren and Madeleine May built this treehouse fort in Massachusetts for their visiting grandsons, Matthew and Toben. The entire family (all three generations) participated in the construction. This is a two-part tree-house, one section on posts and the other on posts and a tree. A solid bridge with rope railing connects them.

Russian River Treehouse

Jim Shaw used our first book (from 1979!) to help him build this treehouse located by the Russian River, north of San Francisco. He later replaced the original stairway with a sturdy rope suspension bridge and eventually he plans to install a metal spiral staircase. The front railing doubles as a launching pad for water balloons!

Surprise Birthday Present

Benjamin and Sebastian Pereira's treehouse was built by their father and his friends as a birthday present. What started out to be a platform in a tree, evolved into a full-fledged treehouse with walls, windows and roof. Once they started building, they couldn't stop until it was a complete tree fort.

Thirty Years of Memories

This weathered treehouse was built for our kids 30 years ago and still holds up during the hurricanes that frequent Long Island. Every spring we inspect it and, if necessary, make repairs, readying it for local kids and nieces and nephews who visit. When our over 6-foot-tall sons come to visit, they make it a point to climb the treehouse stairs and revisit old memories. The space under the treehouse conveniently provides an enclosure for our pool pump.

Spiral Staircase Stronghold

Over a period of 12 months, builder Mark Terry made this 10x12-foot treehouse with gabled roof for his 5-year-old son. It stands on a 14x18-foot platform, 14 feet above the ground. The exterior is cedar shakes with rough redwood trim. All the windows, doors and pine are from left-over construction jobs. He constructed the 7-foot-diameter spiral staircase with a blacksmith friend, purchasing the railing components. The treehouse, which also serves as a guesthouse, is supported by one tree and five poles. The tree weaves in and out of the house in five places. "It is engineered on rolling joints so the treehouse can move independently," Mark says, "and it has survived 75 mph winds."

Minnesota Mini-Home

Caitlyn Strack of Minnesota sent us this photo of her unique playhouse/treehouse supported by posts that Don Ross built for her. The roof gable is covered with pretty scalloped shingles and the round front porch with its wooden railing has plenty of room for a couple of chairs for friends to visit. The siding is painted a bright blue.

Collin's Treehouse
"Collinwood"

Graphic designer Brian Marquis started constructing this treehouse for his son, Collin, by building a model of the tree, followed by a scale model of the treehouse. Using leftover lumber from other building projects, he began construction in the spring. The treehouse was built 18 feet up in the tree where several trunks fanned out to provide space for a platform. Brian strove to make the treehouse "tree-friendly," allowing the many branches to penetrate the platform, walls and roof. He did most of the construction on the ground, hoisting sections up into the tree. He found that using deck screws rather than nails to be practical and time saving.

Three-Tiered Treehouse

Jeff Eames of Long Island, New York, built this treehouse for his daughter, Davis, using leftover wood from his tree-cutting business. He cut the trees into lumber using a portable "Alaskan sawmill." The only cost was for threaded rods that he used to bolt the beams to the trees. He built the treehouse using arborist techniques, riggings and rope.

Treeless Treehouse

If you don't have a tree in your backyard or if your trees don't lend themselves to a traditional treehouse, you can build this treeless treehouse to give you the same feeling of being up in the air in your own special lookout tower. You can order all the materials from your local lumberyard for about $500, and build it in a couple of weekends. It's designed to be easy to build, using as few cuts as possible, and is big enough to support the whole family or invite in the neighborhood kids.

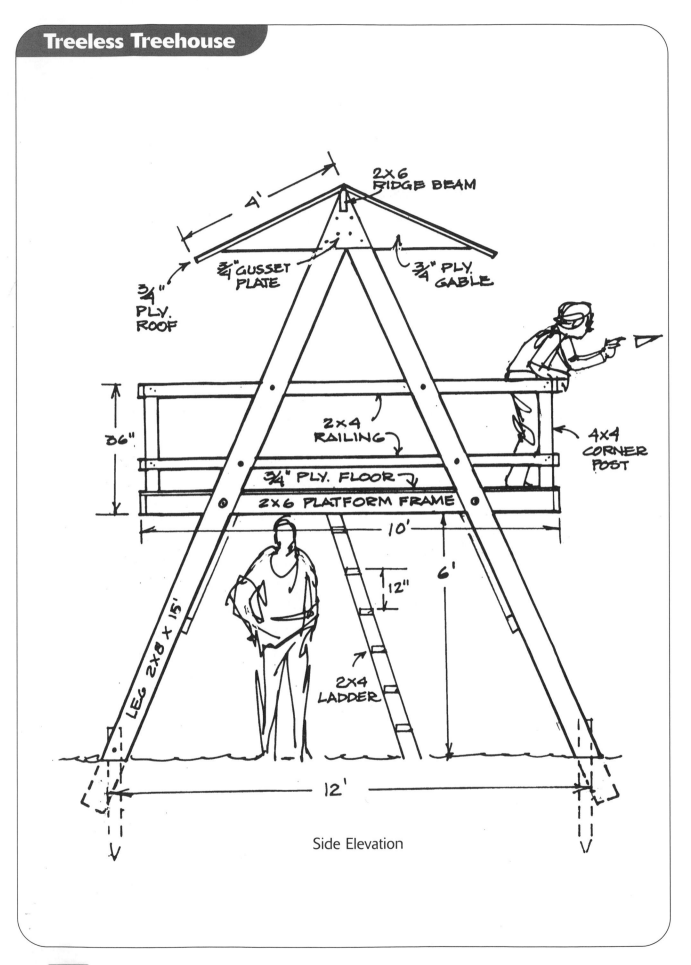

2X6 RIDGE BEAM

4'

¾" GUSSET PLATE

¾" PLY. GABLE

¾" PLY. ROOF

2X4 RAILING

4X4 CORNER POST

36"

¾" PLY. FLOOR

2X6 PLATFORM FRAME

10'

6'

12"

LEG 2X8 X 15'

2X4 LADDER

12'

Side Elevation

✳ Materials List for the Treeless Treehouse

Quantity	Description	Length	Location
(1)	2x4 P.T. lumber	8 feet	stakes
(4)	2x8 P.T. lumber	16 feet	legs
(2)	2x6 #2 pine	10 feet	platform
(6)	2x6 #2 pine	8 feet	platform joists
(1)	2x6 #2 pine	12 feet	ridge beam
(16)	2x6 #2 pine	10 feet	decking
(1)	4x4 #2 cedar	12 feet	corner posts
(2)	2x4 #2 pine	8 feet	braces
(4)	2x4 #2 pine	10 feet	railings
(4)	2x4 #2 pine	8 feet	railings
(3)	3/4-inch ext. plywood	4x8 feet	roof, gussets and gables
(1)	ladder	7 feet tall	
(4)	1/2-inch-dia. galv. bolts	3 1/2 inches	legs to platform
(8)	3/8-inch-dia. galv. bolts	6 inches	posts to platform frame
(1)	cartridge silicone caulk		ridge
3 lbs.	2-inch galv. deck screws		deck and roof
1 lb.	10d galv. common nails		deck

dia. = diameter; ext. = exterior; galv. = galvanized; P.T. = pressure treated

Step 1

Staking Out

Cut and drive four 24-inch stakes into the ground as shown in, leaving 8 inches above the ground. Make sure they are plumb (vertical).

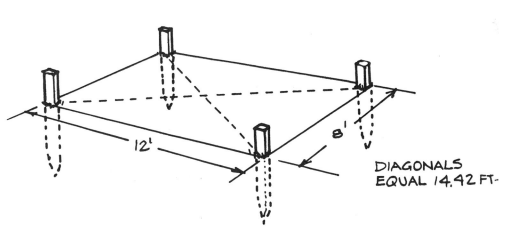

DIAGONALS EQUAL 14.42 FT.

Step 2

Building the Legs

Cut the four 2x8 legs. Cut the gusset plates and gables out of a sheet of 3/4-inch plywood and screw them onto the 16-foot long, 2x8 legs where they join together at the top. Cut $1^1/_2$ x $5^1/_2$-inch notches for the ridge beam to rest in.

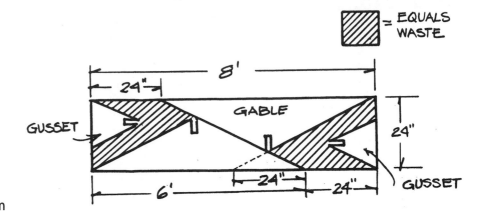

Cutting Plan for Exterior Plywood

Step 3

Building the Platform Frame

Cut six of the 8-foot long 2x6s exactly 93 inches in length. Place them on the ground, parallel to each other, 24 inches apart. Frame them with two 10-foot-long 2x6s, nailing the 10-footers to the 2x6 cross beams (joists), using two 10d nails at each joint. Check to make sure the platform is square by measuring the diagonals. (They should be the same.) Nail a 2x4 diagonally across the platform frame to hold it square.

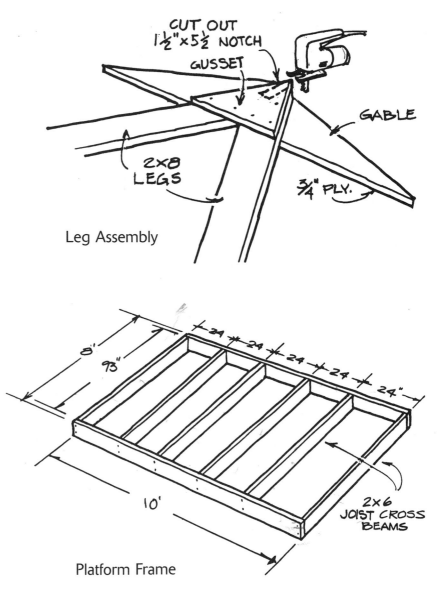

Leg Assembly

Platform Frame

Leg/Ridge Beam Assembly

Step 4

Erecting the Legs

Rarely is the ground perfectly level, so make sure to adjust both pairs of legs so they are level with one another. This can be accomplished by digging out a hole for the legs that rest on the high side of the ground.

With the help of several people, raise the two sets of legs and temporarily brace them together with 2x4s. While standing on a stepladder, slip the 2x6 ridge beam into the pockets and screw them in place. Check to make sure the ridge beam is level. If it isn't, adjust the legs so they are level.

Note:

Although the legs only need to be 15-feet long, an extra 12 inches allows for any leveling that may be necessary.

Step 5

Platform

Use a plumb line to center the platform between the legs. Drill $1/2$-inch-diameter holes, 6 feet up from the ground, through each leg and into the sides of the platform, attaching them with a $1/2$-inch bolt. It is **important** to make sure all four holes are level with each other.

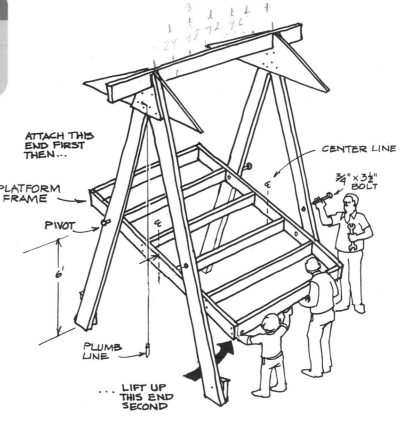

Attaching the Platform

Step 6

Braces

To keep the structure from swaying (racking) from left to right, screw 2x4 braces to the legs and to the platform floor joists at 45-degree angles.

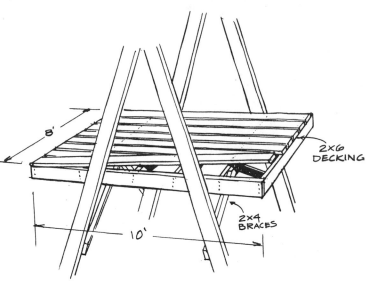

Brace and Decking

Step 7

Deck

Screw 16 pieces of 2x6 decking, each 10-feet long, to the platform frame, attaching them with 2-inch deck screws.

Step 8

Railing Posts

Cut four pieces of 4x4, each 36 inches long for the corner posts. Use an electric jigsaw to cut pocket holes through the deck boards at each corner and bolt the bottom of each post to a corner of the floor frame, using 3/8-inch-diameter bolts.

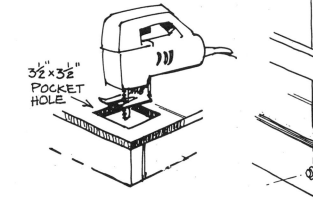

Railing Post Assembly

Step 9

Roof

Screw the two remaining sheets of plywood to the 3/4-inch-thick plywood gables and to the ridge beam. Caulk the seam along the top with silicone caulk.

Roof Overview

The Hobbit Treehouse: Our Story

This Hobbit Treehouse is reminiscent of J.R.R. Tolkien's *Lord of the Rings* trilogy. It is built in a very large tree, using the tree trunk and two branches for support. The house can be pre-built on the ground and hoisted up into the tree in separate pieces. The appeal of this treehouse is its "higgly-piggly" construction. Nothing is built at right angles or level except for the floor. Contrary to what you might think, this makes it hard to build—but worth it!

✳ Materials List for the Hobbit Treehouse

Quantity	Description	Length	Location
Ladder			
(2)	2x6 #2 pine	10 feet	ladder sides
(2)	2x6 #2 pine	10 feet	ladder rungs
Platform Frame			
(2)	2x8 #2 pine	12 feet	frame support beams
(2)	mini-ties	8 feet	floor joists
Decking			
(4)	2 x 9-inch spruce	13 feet	(based on decking for 6x6-foot platform)
Walls			
(2)	mini-ties	8 feet	corner posts
(5)	1/2-inch AC ply.	4x8-foot sheets	sheathing* OR
(16)	1x10 #2 rough pine	12 feet	siding* (*Depending on the size of your treehouse, you may need 2x4 framing before attaching the siding and windows.)
Windows & Doors			
(1)	3/4-inch AC ply.	4x8-foot sheet	2 windows and door
(2)	1x4 T&G cedar	8 feet	casing
(1)	2x3 spruce	8 feet	window hinge
(2)	1x4 cedar	10 feet	door and window trim
(8)	5-inch hanger screws (4 pair)		window hinge
(16)	3/8 x 2-inch carriage bolts		door and windows
Roof			
(2)	2x8 clear cedar	12 feet	roof rafters
(1)	2x6 clear cedar	8 feet	ridgepole
(5)	2 1/2-inch-dia. posts	10 feet	horizontal nailers
2 bundles	18-inch hand-split shakes		roof
Rope Railing			
(1)	1/2-inch-thick manila rope	100 feet	rope railing

AC ply. = A/C-grade exterior plywood; dia. = diameter; nailers = roof boards to which wood shingles are nailed; T&G = tongue and groove

If you love to work in wood

and have plenty of time, this style of treehouse may be just right for you. Be advised that since practically all the joints are at crazy angles, it may take as much as half an hour to join two pieces of wood together properly. Connections to the tree are also painstakingly slow and often have to be carefully carved to conform to the irregular shape of the tree.

We were fortunate to have an almost perfect tree to build in—a large maple, 5 feet wide at the trunk with thick horizontal branches 7 feet up from the ground. You could practically walk from branch to branch without holding on.

Our clients wanted a treehouse for their grandkids—a shelter where they could play protected from the rain and wind with a deck that looked out into the gardens and yard. We wanted to build an inviting treehouse in the tree, not too high up, surrounded by rustling leaves, creating a sense of privacy.

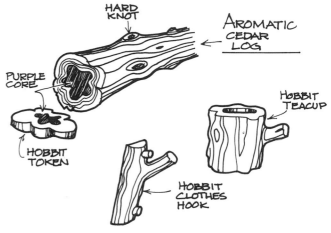

Figure 1

We decided early on to use logs, rather than sawn lumber, to build the two main platforms. Our goal was to make the treehouse look as much a part of the tree as possible. In an ideal world, the treehouse would be made out of the tree's fallen branches, but none were available around this pristine tree.

We used two types of logs for most of the construction: 3x5-inch mini-ties to construct the support framing, and aromatic cedar posts for the railings, etc. *(see Materials List)*. Two exceptions are: the main support beam, built out of two pieces of 2x8 lumber, and the steps, constructed from 2x6 cedar lumber. These could also be made from cedar logs.

We were fortunate to be building in an area where cedar trees are plentiful. Our friends Peggy and Redjeb were building a house and generously offered to give us some of the cedar logs on their property. Since cedar takes years to decay, many of the logs we found lying on the ground had died several years ago and lost their bark, making them smooth and easy to work with. Cedar logs also contain hard knots that if carefully sanded smooth, give the "gnarly" look that we wanted for this design. We were able to purchase additional cedar posts, 3 to 4 inches in diameter, at a nursery wholesale outlet for a very reasonable price and for about half of what a 2x4 would have cost.

This type of cedar is often used to make cedar chests and closets since its aromatic scent keeps the moths away. We crosscut small pieces off tiny branches and used them as secret tokens to enter the hobbit house. We also used pieces of this magical wood, with its purple core, to carve hobbit teacups and clothes hooks for the treehouse interior *(see Figure 1)*.

Building the Hobbit Treehouse

The first thing we installed in the tree was the main support beam that we decided should be hung on two very thick horizontal branches. Luckily, we noticed in advance that these two branches moved several inches with the wind so we used eyebolts to make a flexible connection *(see Figure 2).* Once this was in place, we were able to frame out from the tree, using 3 x 5-inch mini-ties that later support the 2 x 9-inch scaffolding boards.

At this point, to make the remaining construction easier, we built a set of stairs going up to a small platform that leads to the main deck. (One of our readers told us that 90 percent of the time his kids played on the deck rather than inside the tree-

DECK
2" × 9"
SCAFFOLDING
"STAGING"
PLANKS

MAIN
SUPPORT

3×5
MINI TIE

DETAIL

6"×½" EYE SCREW

SHACKLE

9" × ½"
EYE
BOLT

DOUBLE
2×8

DOUBLE
NUTS

BRANCH

SECTION
VIEW

Figure 2: Support Beam

house.) Following the hobbit theme, we built the stairs using no nails or screws—just mortise and tenon joints held together by wooden pegs. (A mortise is a notch cut out in wood to receive a tenon.) This was a labor of love, involving sixteen hand-carved mortises *(see Figure 3).*

After completing the stairs and deck, we built the railings, weaving rope over the top and bottom rails to fill the open area and make it safer. *(See "Making Rope Railings" on page 31–32.)*

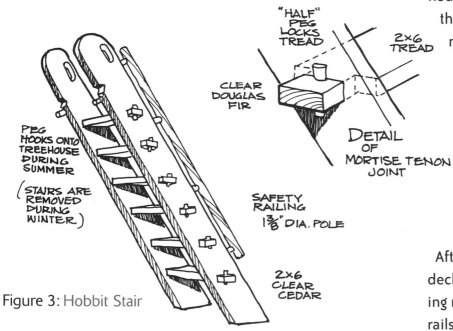

"HALF"
PEG
LOCKS
TREAD

2×6
TREAD

CLEAR
DOUGLAS
FIR

DETAIL
OF
MORTISE TENON
JOINT

PEG
HOOKS ONTO
TREEHOUSE
DURING
SUMMER

(STAIRS ARE
REMOVED
DURING
WINTER.)

SAFETY
RAILING
1⅜" DIA. POLE

2×6
CLEAR
CEDAR

Figure 3: Hobbit Stair

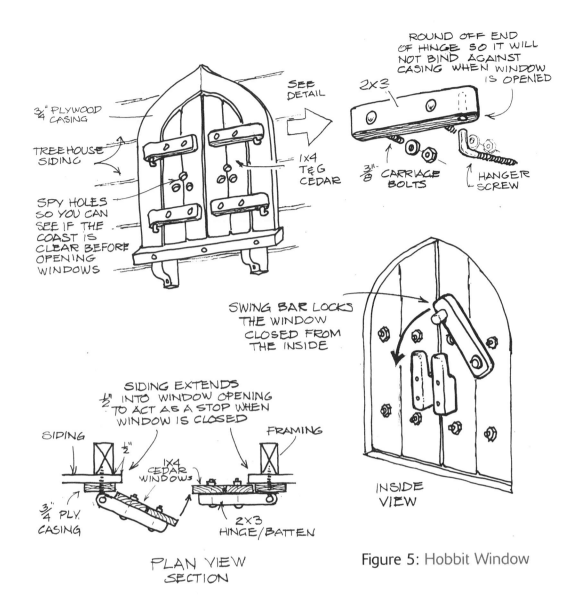

ROUND OFF END OF HINGE SO IT WILL NOT BIND AGAINST CASING WHEN WINDOW IS OPENED

2x3

3/8" CARRIAGE BOLTS

HANGER SCREW

3/4" PLYWOOD CASING

TREEHOUSE SIDING

SPY HOLES SO YOU CAN SEE IF THE COAST IS CLEAR BEFORE OPENING WINDOWS

SEE DETAIL

1x4 T&G CEDAR

SWING BAR LOCKS THE WINDOW CLOSED FROM THE INSIDE

SIDING EXTENDS 1/2" INTO WINDOW OPENING TO ACT AS A STOP WHEN WINDOW IS CLOSED

SIDING

1/2"

1x4 CEDAR WINDOWS

FRAMING

3/4" PLY. CASING

2x3 HINGE/BATTEN

PLAN VIEW SECTION

INSIDE VIEW

Figure 5: Hobbit Window

We settled on having a two-level deck and added hand-made windows *(see Figure 5)* that open out, using a rope/pulley system. If you decide to enclose your sides, we suggest using either $1/2$-inch plywood sheathing or 1x10 rough northern pine siding attached to the corner posts. You can give the siding boards more character by scalloping the edges with a jigsaw and overlapping the boards *(see Figure 6)*.

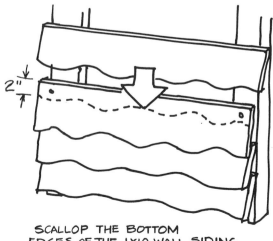

2"

SCALLOP THE BOTTOM EDGES OF THE 1X10 WALL SIDING AND ATTACH IT BY OVERLAPPING THE LOWER BOARD BY 2".

Figure 6: Wall Siding

We wanted the roof to look a bit crooked or "off kilter." We accomplished this by making the left rafters longer than the right rafters and positioned the rear rafters lower, giving the front of the roof a soaring upward look. We decided that the best way to connect the two sets of rafters was using round poles. This provided a surface to nail the hand-split cedar shakes to and gave the roof the curved look that we wanted (see Figure 7).

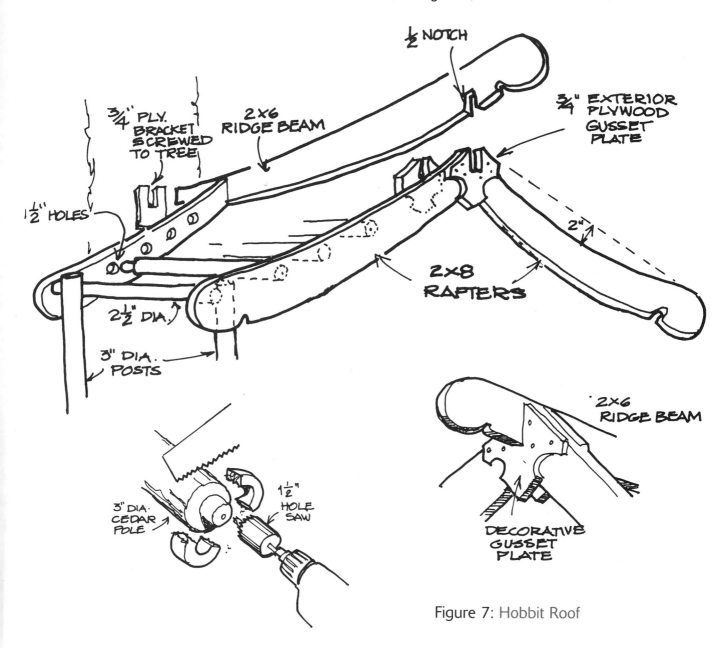

Figure 7: Hobbit Roof

For the final touch, we added an open pediment, made up of curved branches, connected to the front gable. (A pediment is a low gable—typically a triangular portion of wall between the enclosing lines of a sloping roof.)

This project was divided into two phases—the two platforms and the stairs, followed by the treehouse structure. Each phase took about a month to build, working two to three days a week at a leisurely pace.

Four Playhouse Designs

When you are deciding what to build for your kids, consider their ages and how adventuresome they might be. Both playhouses and treehouses are wonderful voyages into the imagination for kids, but for a young child (between one and five years old), a playhouse might be more appropriate. Playhouses are built on the ground and are more easily accessible. They are usually built smaller than treehouses and should be scaled down to accommodate the size of your kids. Because playhouses are on the ground and are smaller than treehouses, they tend to be less expensive (not always true) and easier to build. It is a misconception that playhouses are only popular with girls. We have included designs for playhouses in this book—both the Hobbit House and the Pie-Rat Ship Playhouse—that will appeal equally to boys and girls and supply them with hours of enjoyment.

Some playhouses also have the advantage of being turned into storage spaces or garden sheds once they are outgrown by the kids. One design, the Storage Shed Playhouse, serves both purposes from the beginning. For those who have their heart set on a treehouse, but do not have access to trees, we've included a Treeless Treehouse *(see Chapter 3)*.

"Pie-Rat" Ship Playhouse

Kids love the fantasy associated with a pirate ship. From Peter Pan to Bluebeard, pirate legends live on and what better way to celebrate them than to build this pirate ship playhouse.

Kids can don pirate costumes, practice "pirate speak," and organize a pirate party all centered around this terrific building project.

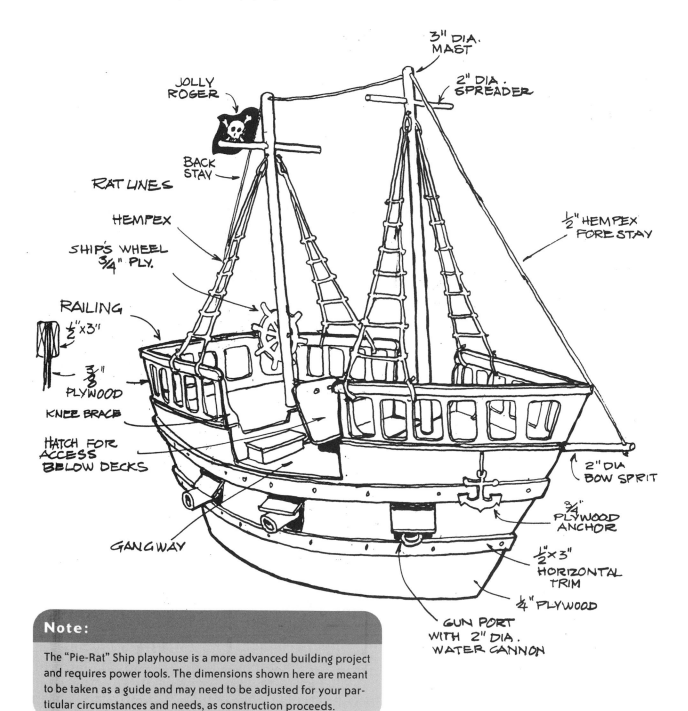

3" DIA. MAST

2" DIA. SPREADER

JOLLY ROGER

BACK STAY

RAT LINES

HEMPEX

SHIP'S WHEEL 3/4" PLY.

RAILING 1/2"x3"

3/8" PLYWOOD

KNEE BRACE

HATCH FOR ACCESS BELOW DECKS

GANGWAY

1/2" HEMPEX FORE STAY

2" DIA BOW SPRIT

3/4" PLYWOOD ANCHOR

1/2"x3" HORIZONTAL TRIM

1/4" PLYWOOD

GUN PORT WITH 2" DIA. WATER CANNON

Note:

The "Pie-Rat" Ship playhouse is a more advanced building project and requires power tools. The dimensions shown here are meant to be taken as a guide and may need to be adjusted for your particular circumstances and needs, as construction proceeds.

A hatch in the deck gives access to both the forward and stern (captain's) quarters. The two masts are rigged with ratline for climbing and keeping a lookout for enemy ships. Ideally, this ship would have moat around it and a removable gangplank.

Building the "Pie-Rat" Ship Playhouse

Step 1   **Making the Strongback**

It is important to start out with a strong, level platform "strongback" on which to construct the boat. This platform is made out of two 2x6s screwed to two saw-horses. Normally, boats are built upside-down during the first stage of construction, but in this case, the ship is built right side up. This avoids having to turn the boat over later, which could damage it.

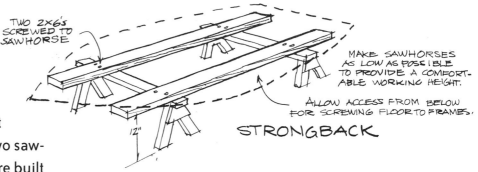

TWO 2X6's SCREWED TO SAWHORSE

MAKE SAWHORSES AS LOW AS POSSIBLE TO PROVIDE A COMFORTABLE WORKING HEIGHT.

ALLOW ACCESS FROM BELOW FOR SCREWING FLOOR TO FRAMES.

12"

STRONGBACK

✳ Materials List for the "Pie-Rat" Ship

Quantity	Description	Length	Location
(1)	2x6 #2 fir	14 feet	strongback
(2)	low sawhorses		
Frame			
(7)	3/4-inch AC ply.	4 x 8-foot sheets	frames, floors and decks
(1)	1x2 #2 pine	12 feet	temporary support
(1)	2x4 #2 fir	4 feet	bow stem
(7)	2x2 #2 cedar	8 feet	stiffeners
Side Panels			
(3)	1/4-inch ext. AC ply.	4 x 8-foot sheets	side panels
Miscellaneous			
(2)	3/8-inch wood dowels	36 inches	gun port, pivot rods
(1)	3/8-inch AC ply.	4 x 8-foot sheets	railings
(3)	1/2 x 3-inch clear cedar	12 feet	handrail and wedge strip
Rigging			
(2)	3-inch-dia. poles clear fir	12 feet	masts
(1)	1 1/2-inch-dia. poles clear fir	6 feet	spreaders
(1)	5/8-inch Hempex rope	150 feet	ratlines (or nylon rope)
Hardware			
1 lb.	galv. screws	1 1/2 inches	
1 lb.	galv. screws	2 inches	
(1)	8 oz. bottle Titebond III glue		
1 gal.	flat black enamel paint		
1 gal.	light oak stain		

AC ply. = A/C-grade exterior plywood; dia. = diameter; gal. = gallon; galv. = galvanized

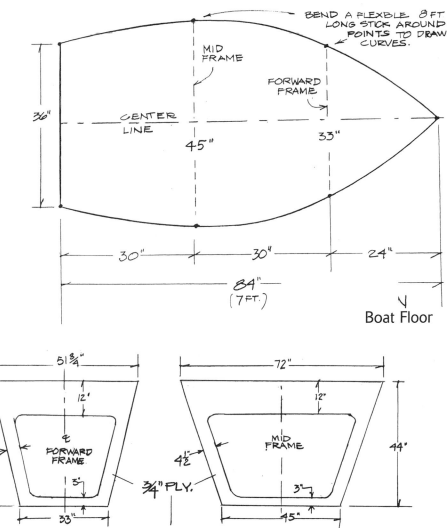

Boat Floor

Step 2

Building the Boat Floor

The boat floor is made out of a 4x8-foot piece of $^3/_4$-inch plywood. Use a thin, flexible, 8-foot-long stick to draw the curves of the boat floor. Using an electric jigsaw, cut out the bottom floor of the boat and temporarily screw it to the 2x6s on the sawhorse. Draw a line down the exact center of the bottom floor. This line will be used as a reference line when positioning the boat frames.

Cut out the forward, mid, and transom frames (and the seat) from another piece of $^3/_4$-inch plywood. Round off and sand smooth the inside edges of the frames to prevent splinters. Cut out a transom window from inside the transom frame and save. Glue and screw the seat to the floor.

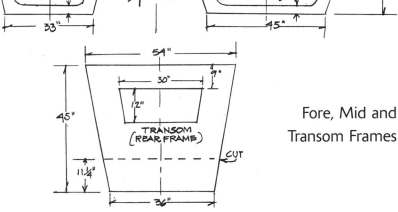

Fore, Mid and Transom Frames

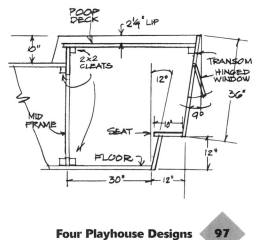

Section through Aft Cabin

Glue and screw the three frames to the bottom floor. To hold the frames in place until the glue has dried, temporarily screw a 1x2 along the top center of each frame. Cut the "stem" (forward support) out of a 2x4 and temporarily

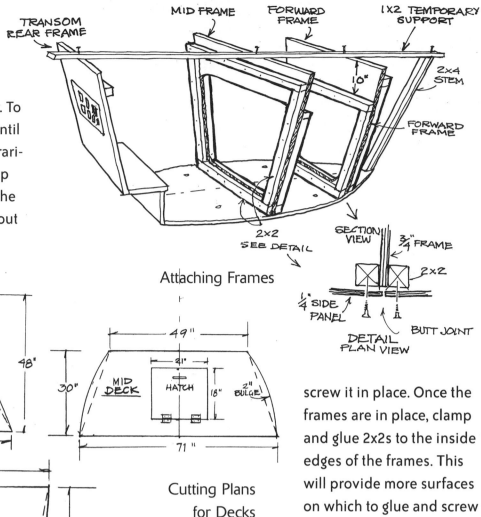

TRANSOM REAR FRAME

MID FRAME

FORWARD FRAME

1X2 TEMPORARY SUPPORT

2X4 STEM

10"

FORWARD FRAME

2X2 SEE DETAIL

Attaching Frames

SECTION VIEW

3/4" FRAME

2X2

1/4" SIDE PANEL

DETAIL PLAN VIEW

BUTT JOINT

FORWARD DECK

3/4" PLY.

2 1/4" BULGE

3" DIA. HOLE

7 1/2"

48"

51"

49"

MID DECK

30"

21"

HATCH

18"

2" BULGE

71"

Cutting Plans for Decks

72"

11"

3" DIA HOLE

POOP DECK (REAR)

3" BULGE

47 1/4"

54"

screw it in place. Once the frames are in place, clamp and glue 2x2s to the inside edges of the frames. This will provide more surfaces on which to glue and screw the 1/4-inch plywood to the frames.

Cut the 3 deck pieces out of 3/4-inch plywood. After the glue holding the frames has dried, remove the 1x2 strip. Glue and screw the deck pieces to the three frames and the front support "stem."

NOTE: THE MID DECK IS 10" BELOW THE FORWARD DECK AND THE REAR (POOP) DECK

POOP DECK (REAR)

MID DECK

FORWARD DECK

3/4" PLY.

3/4" PLY

3/4" PLY

1X2 (TEMPORARY)

10"

2X2

2X4 STEM

STERN (REAR)

45°

3.5

CUT

CUT

2X2s

BOW (FRONT)

ENLARGED VIEW

Installing Decks

Step 3 **Attaching the Boat Sides**

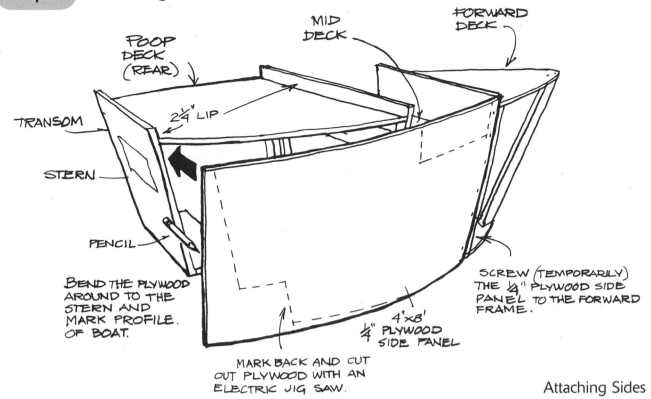

POOP DECK (REAR)

MID DECK

FORWARD DECK

TRANSOM

2¼" LIP

STERN

PENCIL

BEND THE PLYWOOD AROUND TO THE STERN AND MARK PROFILE OF BOAT.

MARK BACK AND CUT OUT PLYWOOD WITH AN ELECTRIC JIG SAW.

4'x8' ¼" PLYWOOD SIDE PANEL

SCREW (TEMPORARILY) THE ¼" PLYWOOD SIDE PANEL TO THE FORWARD FRAME.

Attaching Sides

The boat sides are cut from 3 pieces of $^1/_4$-inch plywood. Hold a piece of $^1/_4$-inch plywood up to one side of the boat, temporarily screwing one end of the plywood to the forward frame and bending the rest of the 4x8-foot panel around the side of the boat. Use a pencil to mark where the plywood panel rests against the deck, the stern, and the bottom of the floor. Follow the same procedure for the other side of the boat and for the two sidepieces at the front of the boat.

Use an electric jigsaw to cut out these pieces, allowing for a $2^1/_2$-inch lip around the top of each sidepiece. The railing is attached to this lip later on *(see page 101)*. Grind and sand down the frames so that the curved sides fit snugly against them, using a block plane and a heavy-duty grinder.

Glue and screw the side panels to the frames on each side, attaching screws every 3 inches. After the sides are attached and sanded smooth, cut out the six 12 x 12-inch gun ports (two in the middle of each section), saving the cut out pieces to be used later as gun port windows.

Note:

It is easier at this point to paint the outside of the hull a flat black and to stain the decks with an oak colored stain.

Step 4 **Trim**

Glue the two $^1/_2$ x 3-inch trim pieces just above and below the gun ports, horizontally along the hull of each side *(see illustration on next page)*.

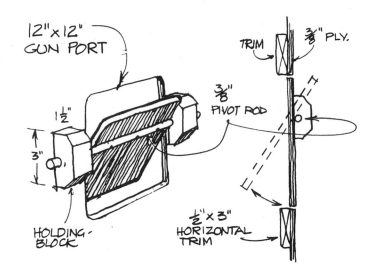

Step 5   Gun-Port Windows

The six gun-port windows can easily be made, using the left-over cutouts. Glue and screw a $^3/_8$-inch-diameter dowel (pivot rod) to the back of each window. Make two "holding blocks" for each window, cut out of a 2x2. Bore a $^3/_8$-inch-diameter hole as close as possible to the inside edge of each holding block (to hold the pivoting dowel). Slip the blocks over the ends of the dowel and glue and screw the blocks to the inside of the hull.

Note:

The pivoting dowel is purposely positioned at the top third of the window for sighting, while the cannon shoots out of the bottom of the window.

Step 6   Water Cannon, optional

The six water cannons are each made out of inexpensive, 2-inch-diameter PVC pipe (bought from any plumbing store), connected with a PVC coupling. Drill a $^1/_2$-inch hole through the center of each coupling and insert a $^1/_2$ x 1-inch bolt from the inside of each hole. Glue one end of each 4-inch pipe to the inside of the coupling. Follow the same process for each water cannon.

Note:

This glue dries very quickly so make sure to glue and insert one piece at a time.

The cannons can be suspended from the underside of the deck, using $^1/_2$-inch mending straps and bolts. The cannons are fired, using a garden hose with a sprayer handle.

Note:

For a special effect, try coating the interior of the pipe with bubble soap.

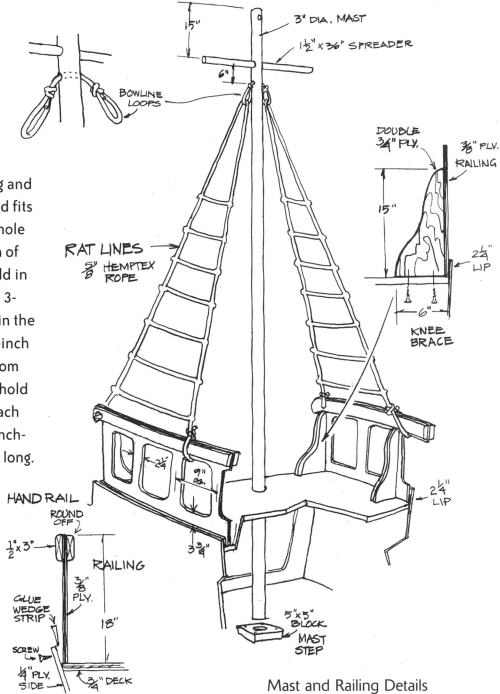

Step 7

Two Masts

Each mast is 11 feet long and 3 inches in diameter and fits into a 3-inch-diameter hole in the deck. The bottom of the mast is stepped (held in place) by a block with a 3-inch diameter hole cut in the middle of it. Drill a 1¹/₂-inch hole, 15 inches down from the top of each mast to hold the "spreader." Make each spreader out of a 1¹/₂-inch-diameter pole, 2¹/₂ feet long. Insert each pole through the hole in each mast, using glue and one screw to secure it.

Note:

If you can't find a 3-inch-diameter pole, you can make the mast out of four pieces of 1x4s, glued together and adjust the size of the deck and block holes accordingly.

Mast and Railing Details

Step 8 Railings

Cut the 15-inch-high railings out of ³/₈-inch plywood and attach them to the ¹/₄-inch-thick plywood sides by inserting a V-shaped spacer (wedge strip) between the railings and the sides. Glue and screw through the side, spacer, and railing, using ³/₄-inch screws. Attach two knee braces to each side, to strengthen the railing. Each brace is made out of two pieces of ³/₄-inch plywood glued together. Strengthen the railing further by gluing and screwing ¹/₂ x 3-inch strips on either side of the railing top.

Drill a ³/₄-inch hole 6 inches below each spreader and insert a ⁵/₈-inch-thick rope through the hole, tying a bowline at each end of the rope. This rope holds the "shrouds" that support the mast. Each shroud is tied to the railing at one end, extends up through the bowline and back down to the railing, where it is tied again. Ratlines are rope ladders that extend up the rigging to the mast. Make them out of ⁵/₈-inch-diameter hemp rope. We recommend using "Hempex" *(see Resources)*, a soft synthetic brown rope.

Start attaching the crosspieces 6 inches above the railing. Each crosspiece should be positioned 8 to 10 inches from the one below it. Allow 5 inches of extra rope at the end of each crosspiece to tie it to the shroud. Separate the loose ends into three strands and melt them, using a propane torch, to keep them from unraveling.

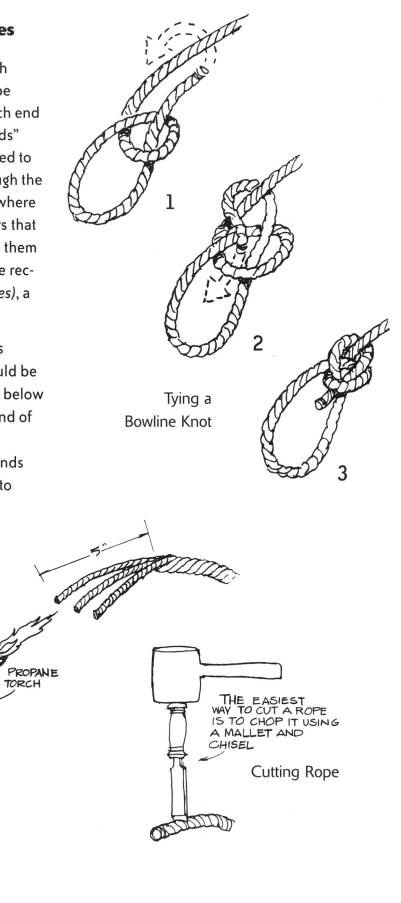

1

2

Tying a
Bowline Knot

3

5"

SEAL THE ENDS OF
SYNTHETIC ROPE BY
MELTING THEM WITH
A PROPANE TORCH.

PROPANE
TORCH

Sealing Nylon Rope

THE EASIEST
WAY TO CUT A ROPE
IS TO CHOP IT USING
A MALLET AND
CHISEL

Cutting Rope

Note:

For Ship's Wheel and Jolly Roger, see Accessories on page 143.

RATLINES - HOW TO JOIN THE HORIZONTAL CROSS ROPES TO THE VERTICAL SHROUDS.

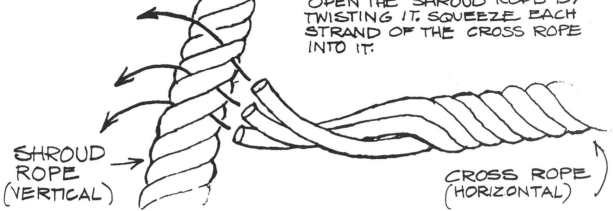

OPEN THE SHROUD ROPE BY TWISTING IT. SQUEEZE EACH STRAND OF THE CROSS ROPE INTO IT.

SHROUD ROPE (VERTICAL)

CROSS ROPE (HORIZONTAL)

In order to attach the crosspieces to the vertical shroud, untwist the rope of the shroud where it will be joined to the crosspiece. Weave the strands of the cross line through the shroud rope. Do this for all three strands on each end of the crosspiece, weaving each strand through a different opening in the shroud rope.

Turn all three loose ends back toward the center of the crosspiece, untwisting the crosspiece rope and weaving the ends of the three strands across and into the crosspiece rope. Further secure the connection by wrapping marine (marlin) line (a strong waxy string) around the final connection and finish it off with a square knot.

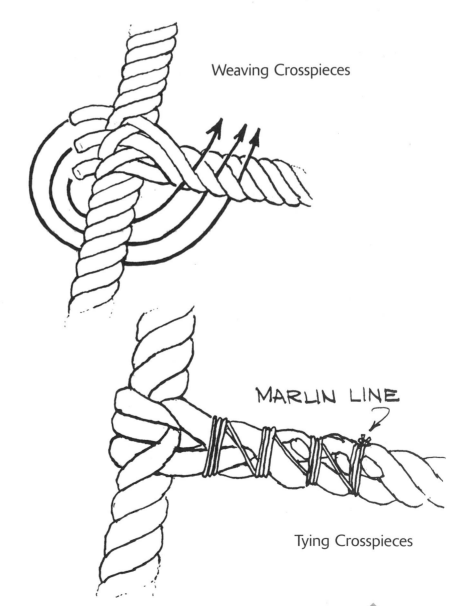

Weaving Crosspieces

MARLIN LINE

Tying Crosspieces

"Pie-Rat" Ship Party

Plan a terrific "Pie-Rat" party. Send out invitations on paper that looks like a pirate's treasure map showing directions to your house along with all the other pertinent information including the date, time, address, and phone number. Make the maps out of brown shopping bag paper and rip the edges to make them look old.

When the guests arrive, give each one a goody bag filled with pirate accessories, such as bandannas, fake mustaches, black eye patches, and long "balloon" swords, etc. Also, give them a list of pirate expressions (see Pirate Speak) to use, such as "Shiver me timbers," "Avast thar matie!" and "Arrrgggh!" If you run out of pirate expressions, just remember to use any words that have "rrrrrs" in them and begin and end your sentences with arrrgggh!"

Tip:

Read these pirate expressions to all the pirate party guests and give a prize to the person who can remember most of them.

Organize a treasure hunt with riddles to decipher and clues hidden at secret points. Sample clue: "Where does the 4-legged ship mascot spend his nights?" Answer: In the doghouse. At the end of the hunt, have a treasure chest or even a box buried in some hidden but accessible spot. Bury the treasure so it can easily be located by cross-referencing two or more landmarks. Place a shovel at the next-to-last clue. Fill the treasure box with gold-wrapped chocolate coins (dubloons) sold at most candy stores.

Instead of the usual cake, serve your "pie-rat" guests blueberry pie decorated with a skull and crossbones crust. For more pirate stuff, visit www.piratestore.com, where you can buy a pirate flag (called Jolly Roger), hats, costumes, maps, and treasure chests.

✳ Pirate Speak

Pirate Expression	Translation
Landlubber	Person who has never been to sea
Scurvy Dog	Scallywag, bad person
Pipe down	Shut up
Arrrgggh!	What the heck? Well . . . etc.
Batten down the hatches	Tie down the doors
Thar she blows	Expression used when a whale is sighted
Hey, ho, blow the man down	Pirate song
Ahoy thar Matie	Hello
Shiver me timbers!	Holy Cow!
Heave ho	Push or pull hard
Clap that man in irons	Arrest that man
Hoist the Jolly Roger	Pull up the pirate's flag
Permission to come aboard	May I get on the ship?
Weigh the anchor	Pull up the anchor
Cap'ns quarters	Captain's room
All hands on deck	Everybody on deck
Avast	What's up? What's happening?
Swab, lad, matie, bloke, hand	Terms for a sailor
Beat to quarters!	Man your battle stations!

Victorian Playhouse

This Victorian (or traditional) playhouse is a perfect size for kids from ages one to eight. The door is only 4 feet high, yet still wide enough for an adult to go through in case of an emergency. One significant feature of this playhouse is a sleeping loft, reached by a ladder and a working window that can be opened to talk with folks below. Another feature is a covered front porch where kids can sit with friends.

With the exception of the pressure-treated base and the 2x6 rafters, the majority of the lumber used to build the Victorian Playhouse is light-weight (and inexpensive) 2x3s and $1/2$-inch ply-wood *(see Figures 1–4)*. The walls can easily be fabricated on the ground and screwed together at the site. This makes it a good project to build in the basement over the winter and install in the spring. The wood for the windows and door are cut out of plywood panels and later hinged to the trim. We recommend covering the roof with cedar shingles, but they can be expensive. To save money, use asphalt shingles, which will also look fine.

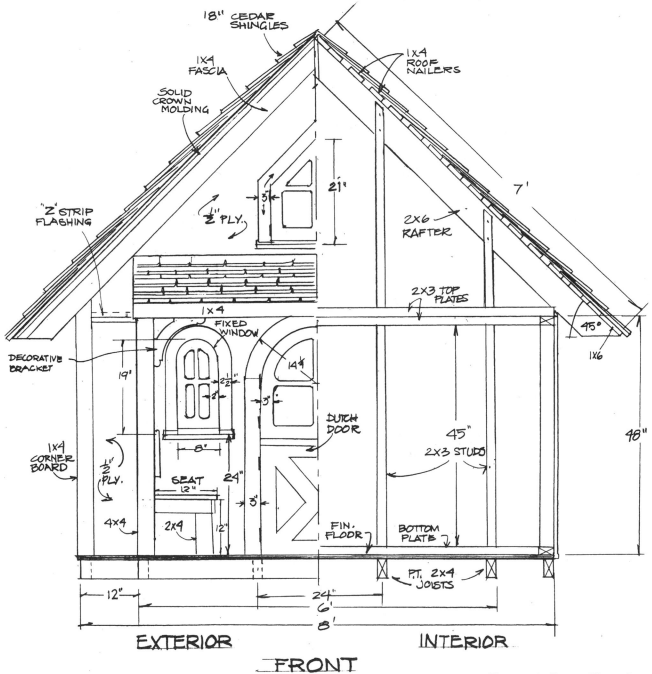

Figure 1: Front Elevation

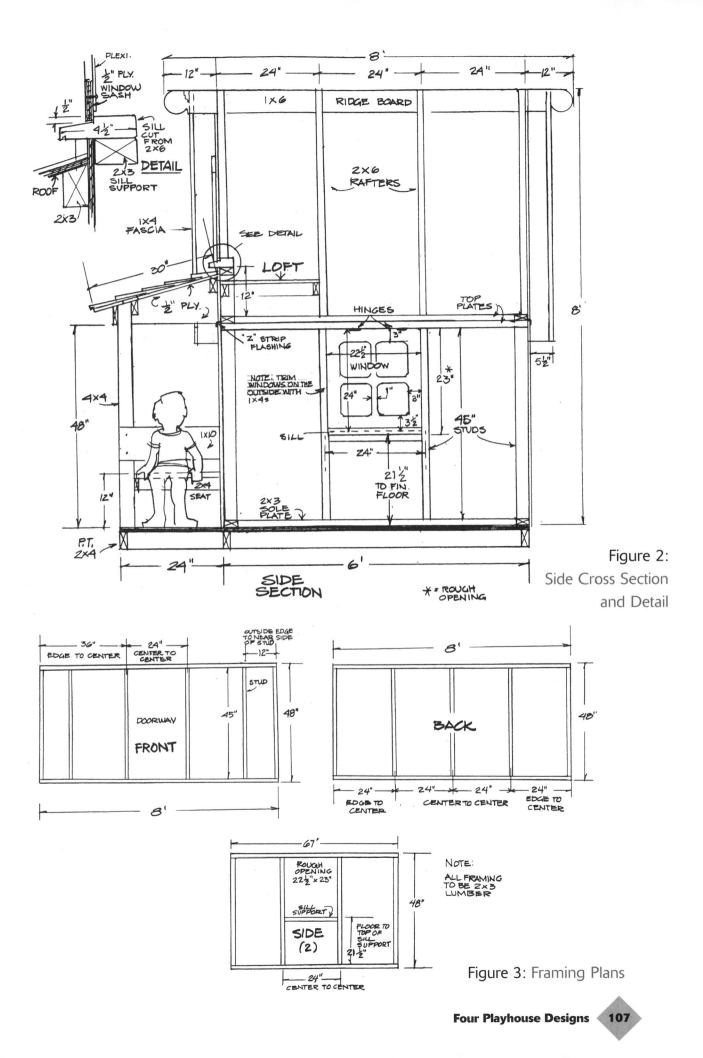

DETAIL

PLEXI.
½" PLY.
WINDOW SASH
½"
4½"
SILL CUT FROM 2×6
2×3 SILL SUPPORT
ROOF
2×3

1×6   RIDGE BOARD

2×6 RAFTERS

1×4 FASCIA

SEE DETAIL

30"

LOFT

½" PLY.

12"

"Z" STRIP FLASHING

NOTE: TRIM WINDOWS ON THE OUTSIDE WITH 1×4s

TOP PLATES

8'

5½"

HINGES

22½"
WINDOW
3"

23"
*

24"
1"

2"

3½"

45" STUDS

4×4

48"

1×10

SILL

21½" TO FIN. FLOOR

24"

SEAT
2×4

12"

2×3 SOLE PLATE

P.T. 2×4

24"   6'

SIDE SECTION

* = ROUGH OPENING

12" 24" 24" 24" 12"
8'

Figure 2:
Side Cross Section and Detail

36" EDGE TO CENTER   24" CENTER TO CENTER   OUTSIDE EDGE TO NEAR SIDE OF STUD 12"

STUD

DOORWAY
45"
48"

FRONT

8'

8'

BACK

48"

24" EDGE TO CENTER   24" CENTER TO CENTER   24" CENTER TO CENTER   24" EDGE TO CENTER

67"

ROUGH OPENING 22½" × 23"

SILL SUPPORT

SIDE (2)

FLOOR TO TOP OF SILL SUPPORT 21½"

48"

NOTE:
ALL FRAMING TO BE 2×3 LUMBER

24" CENTER TO CENTER

Figure 3: Framing Plans

Four Playhouse Designs 107

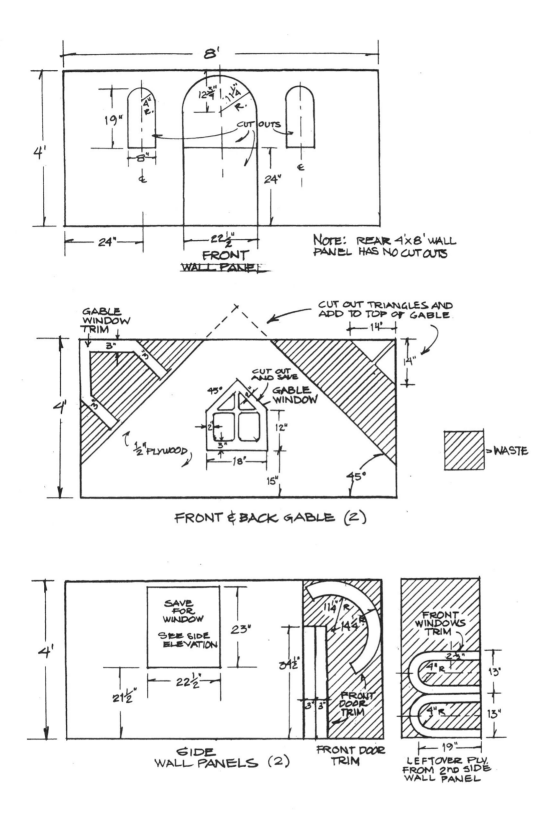

Figure 4: Cutting Diagram for ½-Inch Plywood

❋ Materials List for the Victorian Playhouse

Quantity	Description	Length	Location
Base			
(6)	2x4 P.T. lumber	6 feet	
(4)	2x4 P.T. lumber	8 feet	
(2)	³/₄-inch AC ply.	4 x 8-foot sheets	
Walls			
(12)	2x3 #2 spruce	8 feet	wall studs
(6)	2x3 #2 spruce	8 feet	front/back wall plates
(6)	2x3 #2 spruce	6 feet	side wall plates
(2)	2x3 #2 spruce	10 feet	side window framing
(6)	¹/₂-inch AC ply.	4 x 8-foot sheets	4 walls, window trim
Roof			
(1)	4x4 cedar post	14 feet	porch and loft
(2)	2x4 #2 fir	14 feet	porch roof
(1)	1x6 #2 pine	6 feet	1st porch roof nailer
(4)	1x4 #2 pine	6 feet	spaced porch roof nailers
(8)	2x6 #2 fir	7 feet	rafters
(1)	1x6 #2 pine	10 feet	ridge beam
(3)	1x6 #2 pine	7 feet	1st eave roof nailers
(24)	1x4 #2 pine	7 feet	spaced roof nailers
(2)	decorative braces	14 inches	porch front
(2)	¹¹/₁₆ x 1³/₈-inch molding	14 feet	gable trim
2 squares	18-inch cedar shingles		roof
Loft			
(2)	2x4 #2 fir	8 feet	loft supports
(3)	1x8 #2 pine	10 feet	loft
(1)	⁵/₈-inch-dia. nylon rope	14 feet	loft
Trim			
(4)	1x4 #2 pine	7 feet	gable fascias
(1)	1x4 #2 pine	10 feet	porch fascia
(2)	1x4 #2 pine	6 feet	window frames
(1)	2x6 #2 fir	6 feet	windowsills
(14)	1x4 #2 pine	5 feet	corner trim
Hardware			
(12)	1 x 2-inch galv. butt hinges	(6 pair)	
(2)	¹/₈-inch Plexiglas	2 x 4-foot sheets	windows
2 pieces	Z-strip metal flashing		front and rear walls
1 box	1-inch galv. finishing nails		

AC ply. = A/C-grade exterior plywood; galv. = galvanized; P.T. = pressure treated

Building the Victorian Playhouse

Step 1   Building the Base

Begin by building the base, using pressure-treated 2x4 lumber. Use two 10d galvanized nails in each joint and cover the base with ³/₄-inch AC plywood, nailed down with 2-inch deck nails. You will find that the

4 x 8-foot panels of plywood will automatically "square up" the base frame.

Before proceeding to the next step, level the base by placing bricks or rocks under any low points. Fill in any spaces between the base and the ground with additional rocks or compacted earth to both provide a level platform, and to prevent animals from crawling underneath. During the rest of construction, it is important to keep checking that the base has remained level and has not settled.

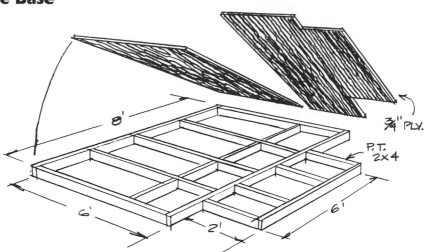

Base with Plywood Flooring

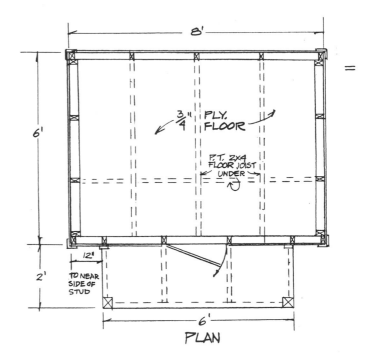

PLAN

Base Framing Plan

Step 2   Building the Wall Frame

The next step is to build the framing for the walls. The best way to do this is to use the floor platform that you have just built as a large worktable. Begin by framing the front and back walls. They should extend to line up with the outside edge of the floor platform. Allow for

the thickness of the front and back walls when you are framing the two sidewalls. You will also notice in Framing Plans on page 108 that the front wall is framed differently than the rear wall because of the door opening.

Once all the walls are framed with 2x3s, you have a choice of erecting them and screwing them together or leaving them on the ground and attaching the $^1/_2$-inch plywood to the frame. We think the latter choice is preferable because it is easier to rest each wall on a pair of sawhorses, allowing you to do the marking and cutting more comfortably. If you use this method, it's a good idea to temporarily raise and test fit the wall framing and then take it down. Use a 4-foot T-square to mark the cuts and an electric jigsaw to cut out the windows and doors. Try to do this as carefully as possible since the cutouts are used later.

Step 3 **Erecting the Walls**

With the help of another person, tilt the walls up and screw them together, using 3-inch galvanized screws. Screw the bottom plate of each wall to the plywood floor. Next, add a top plate to the top of each of the four walls, making sure to overlap the underlying joint at each corner. This top plate will be the base onto which the two gable walls are attached.

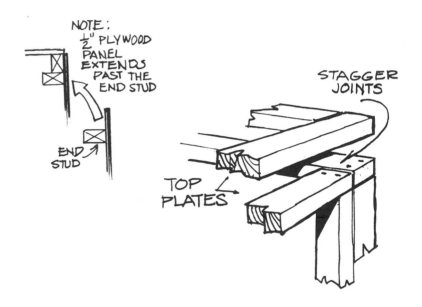

NOTE:
$^1/_2$" PLYWOOD PANEL EXTENDS PAST THE END STUD

END STUD

STAGGER JOINTS

TOP PLATES

Corner Details

Step 4 **Erecting the Ridge Board**

The ridge board has to be put into position before the rafters can be installed. To do this, erect two temporary posts to hold the two ends of the ridge beam. Position the posts so they can hold the ridge beam in the exact center of the playhouse. *See illustrations on next page.*

Step 5   Installing the Rafters

To make construction of the roof easier, we have designed the roof to slope at a 45-degree angle. To make the 8 rafters, cut off each end of a 7-foot-long 2x6 at a 45-degree angle.

Hold one rafter up to the ridge board and mark where the rafter meets the top edge of the top plate. Cut a 1 x 1-inch notch (bird's mouth) in the bottom of the rafter. Hold it up again and, if necessary, adjust the notch so that it fits onto the top plate. Use this rafter as a template to mark the other seven rafters. Screw the rafters to the ridge board and the top plate, using 3-inch screws. Remove the temporary posts.

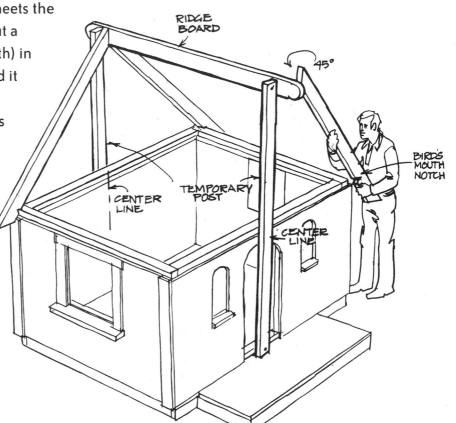

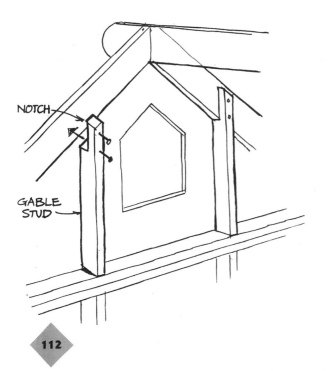

Step 6   Gable Walls

The 2x3 studs for the gabled walls should line up with the wall studs below. You will need to make a notch at the top of the studs where they meet the rafters. Temporarily hold the stud in position and mark where it meets the rafter. Then take it down and cut the notch, using an electric jigsaw. Cut the $1/2$-inch plywood as shown on the cutting plan and nail it to the studs, rafters, and top plate. Both gable panels are identical.

Step 7 Building the Roof

Before installing the shingles, nail a 1x4 gable fascia board to the ends of the nailers. Then add a solid crown molding to the top edge of the fascia *(see Figure 10)*. The cedar shingles are supported by 1x4 nailers (spaced sheathing). The first nailer is a 1x6. The remaining nailers are all 1x4s, spaced 2 inches apart. Cut the nailers 7-feet-long to extend 6 inches past the front and back of the playhouse.

We recommend using 18-inch #1 Perfection select red cedar shingles. If you want to get fancy, you can buy cedar shingles with scalloped bottom edges. If this becomes too expensive, make your own shingles by cutting 18-inch x 7-foot-long strips of exterior plywood, scalloping the edges with an electric jigsaw, and nailing them to the 1x4 nailers. In either case, make sure that the sharp ends of the nails don't extend through to the inside of the playhouse, as this could injure a child's head. (Use 1-inch-long staples if necessary.)

The first row of shingles is always double, followed by rows spaced 5 1/2 inches from the preceding row. As you are shingling, check often to make sure the rows will end up straight at the top. At the top of the roof, run the shingles horizontally along the ridge, alternately overlapping them.

Step 8 Porch

Build the porch using 4x4 cedar for the posts. Build the roof of the porch in the same manner as the main roof using 2x4s and 1x4 nailers.

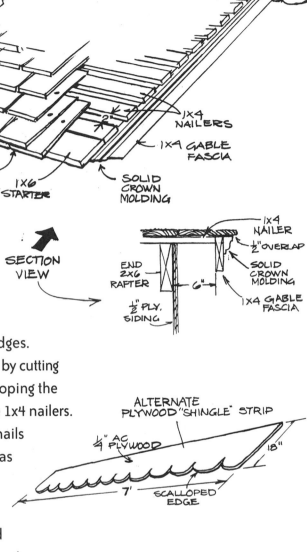

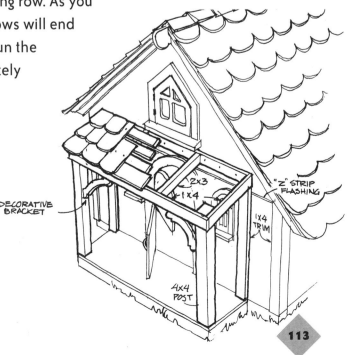

Step 9 Loft

Nail two 2x4s across the interior to support the loft. Measure, cut to fit, and nail 1x8 boards on top of the 2x4s to make the loft. You can access the loft by a 6-foot ladder (not included in Materials List). Attach two 4x4 posts to the open side of the loft, connecting them with ⁵/₈-inch nylon rope as a safety guard. Cushion the loft flooring by covering the loft boards with scrap carpet or a 2-inch foam mattress.

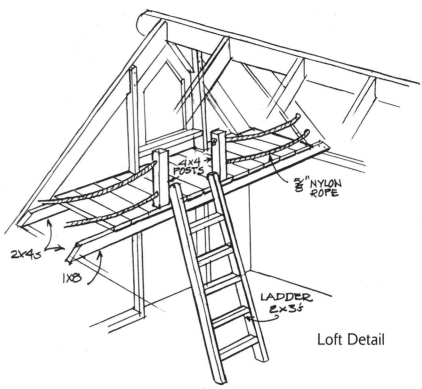

Loft Detail

Step 10 Windows and Door

We designed the windows and door to be made out of the leftover pieces of ¹/₂-inch plywood wall panels, saving both time and money. Using an electric jigsaw, cut out the window openings and screw a piece of ¹/₄-inch Plexiglas (acrylic) to the back. Sand and round off any rough edges to avoid splinters later on, as these windows will be opened and closed frequently.

Cut out the trim pieces from the left-over plywood *(see Cutting Plans on page 108)* and hinge the windows and door to them. Glue and nail the window trim (with the windows attached) to the walls using 1-inch finishing nails. At the bottom of the window trim, attach a sill cut from a 2x6 and slant it to shed rain *(see Detail on page 107)*.

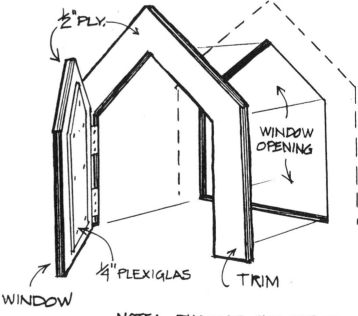

NOTE: PLYWOOD CUT OUT OF WINDOW OPENING USED TO MAKE WINDOW. DITTO FOR DOOR.

114

Hobbit Playhouse

Like the Hobbit Treehouse, this playhouse was inspired by the architecture of the Hobbit houses in the *Lord of the Rings* trilogy, written during the mid-1900s. Although it is not an exact copy of a "Hobbit" house that is built into the ground and has a circular door, we feel that our design reflects the spirit of a Hobbit dwelling with its curved roof and "funky" windows.

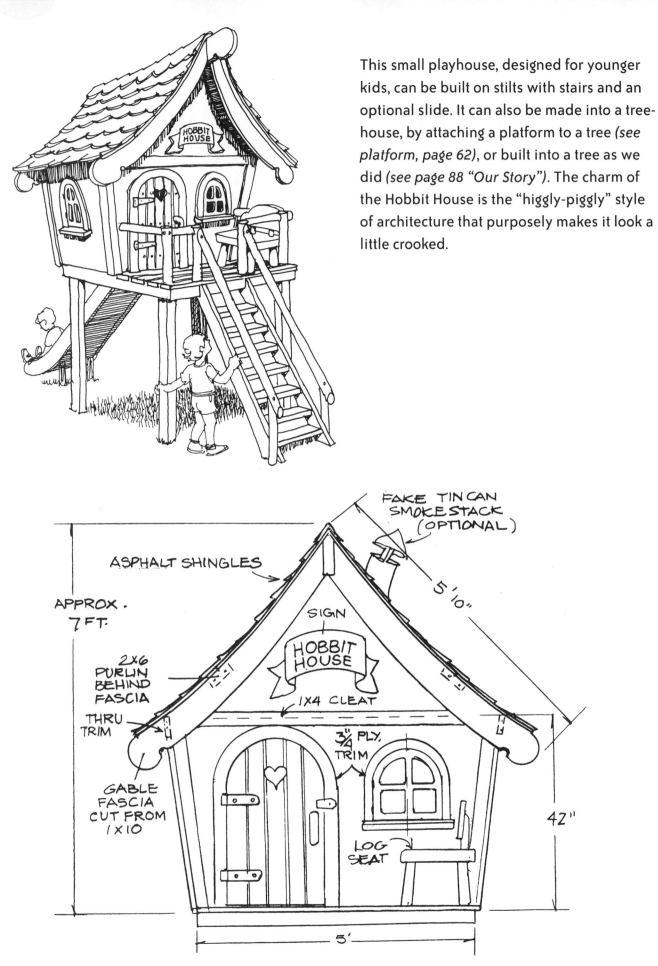

This small playhouse, designed for younger kids, can be built on stilts with stairs and an optional slide. It can also be made into a treehouse, by attaching a platform to a tree *(see platform, page 62)*, or built into a tree as we did *(see page 88 "Our Story")*. The charm of the Hobbit House is the "higgly-piggly" style of architecture that purposely makes it look a little crooked.

FAKE TIN CAN
SMOKE STACK
(OPTIONAL)

ASPHALT SHINGLES

APPROX.
7 FT.

5' 10"

SIGN

HOBBIT
HOUSE

2×6
PURLIN
BEHIND
FASCIA

1×4 CLEAT

THRU
TRIM

3/4" PLY,
TRIM

GABLE
FASCIA
CUT FROM
1×10

42"

LOG
SEAT

5'

Front Elevation

The door is 3 feet high and 2 feet wide, making it a perfect size for kids, but still wide enough that adults can get through in an emergency. To keep it simple, there are no rafters or wall studs in this playhouse; instead it uses plywood and 1x4 cleats or stiffeners to reinforce it. The curve of the roof is made by bending the 1/4-inch plywood and attaching it to the curved edge of the front and rear walls and the curved fascias. The roof is covered with individually cut asphalt shingles, glued with roofing cement, and held in place with staples, although it could also be covered with thatch. The windows, window frames, and door are made from leftover pieces of 3/4-inch plywood. The log bench, emergency escape hatch, and house sign are optional.

❉ Materials List for the Hobbit Playhouse

Quantity	Description	Length	Location
Base			
(4)	2x4 P.T. lumber	6 feet	base
(2)	2x4 P.T. lumber	5 feet	base
Decking			
(8)	5/4x4 decking	5 feet	decking
Floor (front & back)			
(4)	3/4-inch AC ply.	4 x 8-foot sheets	
Sides & Roof			
(4)	1/4-inch AC ply.	4 x 8-foot sheets	
Cleats & Stiffeners			
(10)	1x4 #2 pine	8 feet	
(3)	1x4 #2 pine	12 feet	
Purlins			
(1)	2x6 #2 fir	10 feet	
Fascias			
(2)	1x10 clear cedar or pine	12 feet	
Window Sills			
(1)	2x4 P.T. lumber	6 feet	
Roofing			
2 bundles	asphalt shingles		
Ridge Beam			
(1)	2x8 fir	8 feet	
Hardware			
1 box	3/8-inch staples		
1 gal.	roofing cement		
(3)	1/2 x 2-inch butt hinges		windows
(1)	door handle		
(2)	6-inch strap hinges (1 pair)		
(1)	1/8-inch Plexiglas	1 x 3-foot sheet	(optional for windows)
(1)	1 x 2-inch butt hinges		(optional for escape door)

AC ply. = A/C-grade exterior plywood; gal. = gallon; P.T. = pressure treated

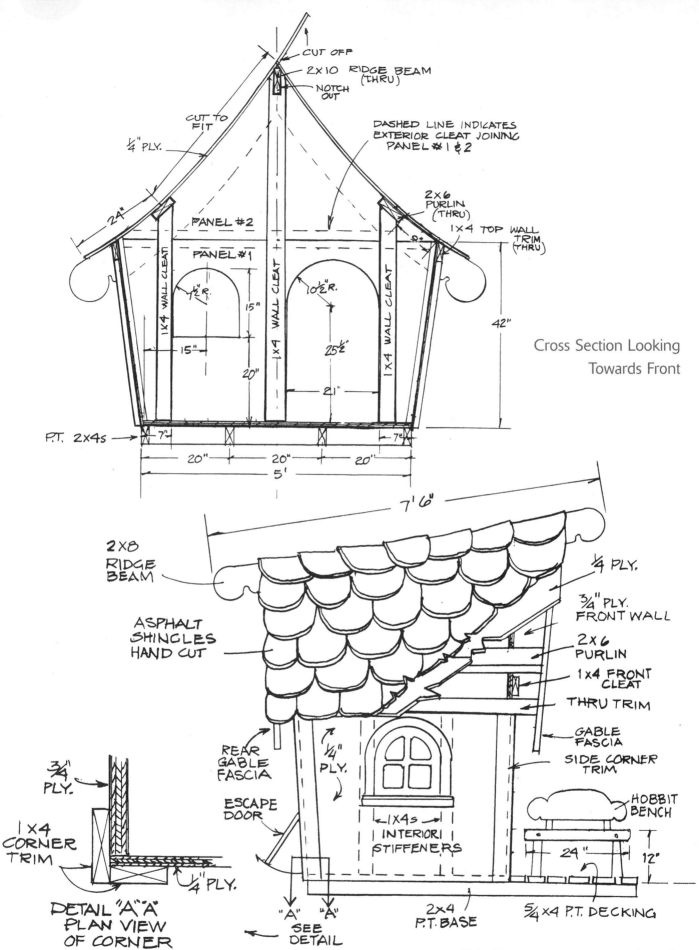

Cross Section Looking Towards Front

CUT OFF
2X10 RIDGE BEAM (THRU)
NOTCH OUT
CUT TO FIT
¼" PLY.
DASHED LINE INDICATES EXTERIOR CLEAT JOINING PANEL #1 & 2
24"
PANEL #2
PANEL #1
1X4 WALL CLEAT
½" R.
15"
15"
1X4 WALL CLEAT
10½" R.
25½"
20"
21"
2X6 PURLIN (THRU)
1X4 TOP WALL TRIM (THRU)
9"
1X4 WALL CLEAT
42"
P.T. 2X4s
7"
7"
20"
20"
20"
5'

2X8 RIDGE BEAM
7' 6"
¼ PLY.
¾" PLY. FRONT WALL
2X6 PURLIN
1X4 FRONT CLEAT
THRU TRIM
GABLE FASCIA
SIDE CORNER TRIM
ASPHALT SHINGLES HAND CUT
REAR GABLE FASCIA
ESCAPE DOOR
¼" PLY.
HOBBIT BENCH
1X4s INTERIOR STIFFENERS
24"
12"
"A" "A"
SEE DETAIL
2X4 P.T. BASE
5/4 X4 P.T. DECKING

¾" PLY.
1X4 CORNER TRIM
¼" PLY.
DETAIL "A""A" PLAN VIEW OF CORNER

Side Elevation and Corner Details

118

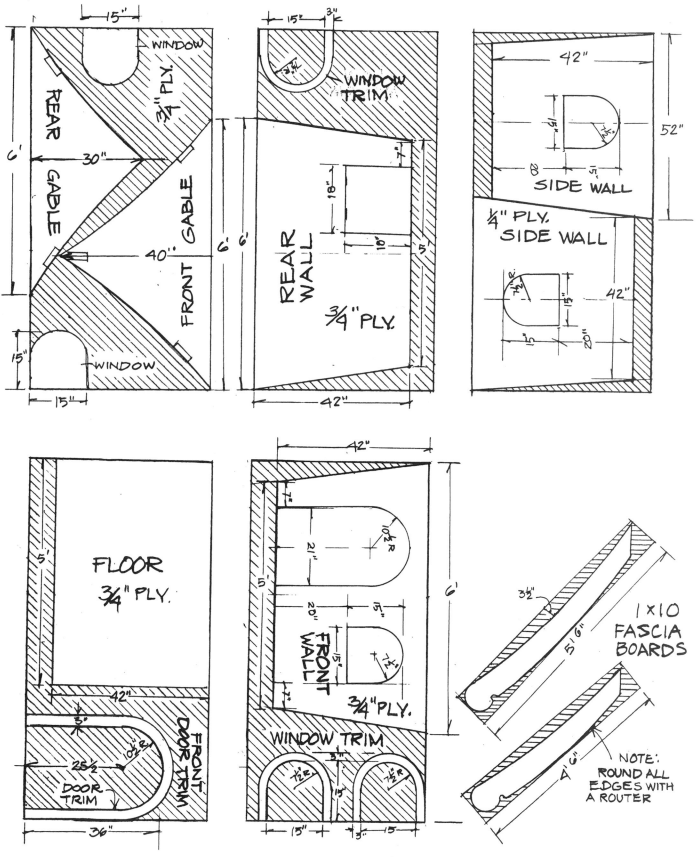

Hobbit Playhouse Cutting Plans

Building the Hobbit Playhouse

Step 1 **Building the Frame**

Cut out all the plywood pieces *(as shown on page 119)* using an
electric jigsaw. Frame the base, using pressure-treated 2x4s.
Cover 42 inches of the floor frame with $^3/_4$-inch plywood and
30 inches of the frame with $^5/_4$x4 decking.

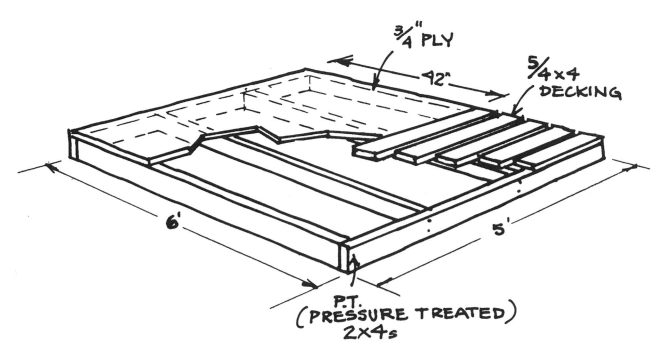

$^3/_4$" PLY

42"

$^5/_4$x4 DECKING

6'

5'

P.T.
(PRESSURE TREATED)
2x4s

Hobbit Playhouse Base Diagram

Join the top and bottom
wall pieces together by
gluing and screwing a
1x4 cleat to them. Glue
and screw three 1x4
vertical wall cleats to
the backside of the
front wall. Do the same
for the back wall.

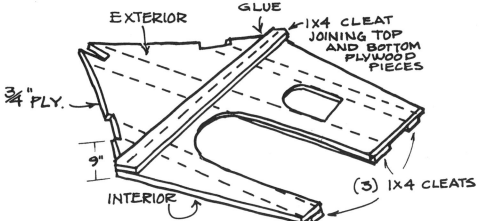

EXTERIOR

GLUE

1X4 CLEAT
JOINING TOP
AND BOTTOM
PLYWOOD
PIECES

$^3/_4$" PLY.

9"

INTERIOR

(3) 1X4 CLEATS

Wall Cleating

Set up the front and rear walls. Attach the walls to the ridge beam and the two purlins. (Purlins are longitudinal beams in the roof frame.) Glue and screw 1x4 stiffeners to the interior sides of the walls next to the windows.

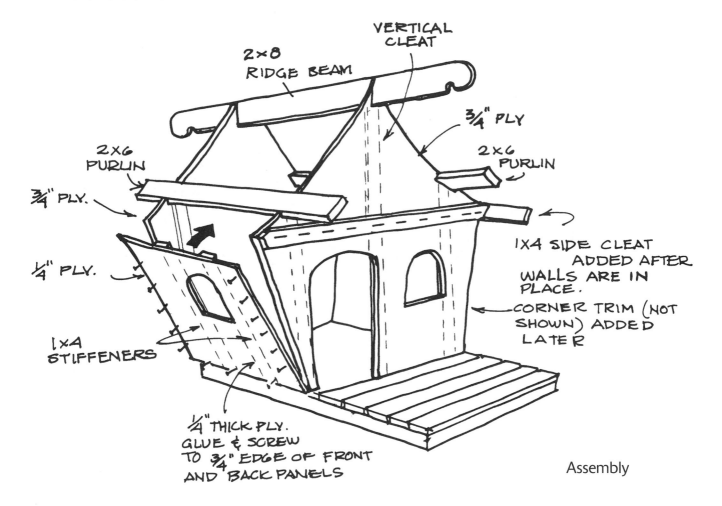

VERTICAL CLEAT

2×8 RIDGE BEAM

¾" PLY

2×6 PURLIN

2×6 PURLIN

¾" PLY.

¼" PLY.

1X4 SIDE CLEAT ADDED AFTER WALLS ARE IN PLACE.

CORNER TRIM (NOT SHOWN) ADDED LATER

1X4 STIFFENERS

¼" THICK PLY. GLUE & SCREW TO ¾" EDGE OF FRONT AND BACK PANELS

Assembly

Step 2 Constructing the Roof

Place a 4 x 8-foot sheet of ¼-inch-thick plywood on the roof of the playhouse so that the bottom edge covers one-half of the 2x6 purlin. Make a mark 2 inches above the ridge beam and cut off the excess plywood. Glue and screw the plywood to the purlin, front and rear walls, and ridge beam.

Cut another sheet of ¼-inch-thick plywood in half lengthwise. Glue and screw it to the remaining half of the

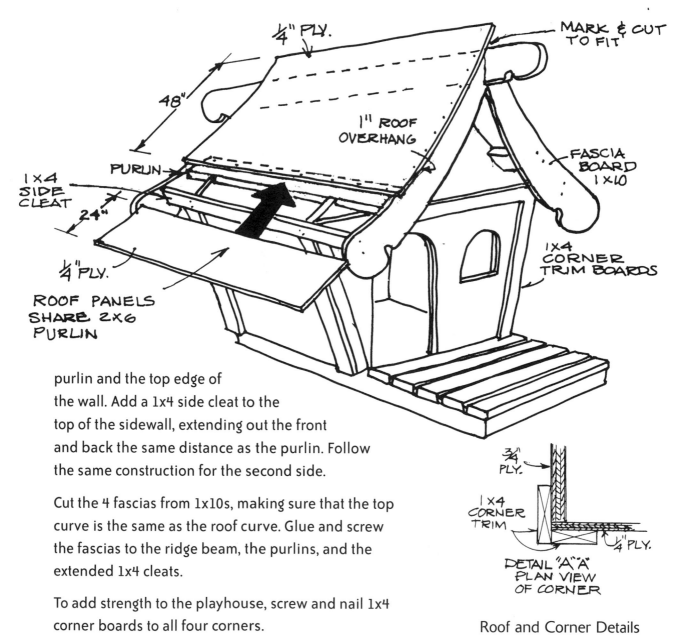

FASCIA BOARDS ARE GLUED AND SCREWED TO RIDGE BEAM, PURLIN AND 1X4 SIDE CLEAT.

¼" PLY.

MARK & CUT TO FIT

48"

1" ROOF OVERHANG

FASCIA BOARD 1 X 10

PURLIN

1 X 4 SIDE CLEAT

24"

¼" PLY.

1 X 4 CORNER TRIM BOARDS

ROOF PANELS SHARE 2X6 PURLIN

¾" PLY.

1 X 4 CORNER TRIM

¼" PLY.

DETAIL "A" "A" PLAN VIEW OF CORNER

purlin and the top edge of the wall. Add a 1x4 side cleat to the top of the sidewall, extending out the front and back the same distance as the purlin. Follow the same construction for the second side.

Cut the 4 fascias from 1x10s, making sure that the top curve is the same as the roof curve. Glue and screw the fascias to the ridge beam, the purlins, and the extended 1x4 cleats.

To add strength to the playhouse, screw and nail 1x4 corner boards to all four corners.

Roof and Corner Details

Step 3   **Covering the Roof**

This playhouse can be covered with several different types of roofing (even thatch); however, because the roof is curved, one of the easiest and least expensive solutions is to use asphalt shingles. They come in a large assortment of colors.

Use tin snips to round off the bottom corners of each shingle, making a scalloped edge. Starting at the bottom, attach each shingle with roofing cement and staples. Make sure the staples do not penetrate through the $1/4$-inch plywood where they could scratch someone's head. Since the roof slants up in the front, you will have to adjust the spacing of each row as you work towards the top. When you reach the ridge, cut the shingles for the top row into 12 x 12-inch pieces and fold them over the roof ridge.

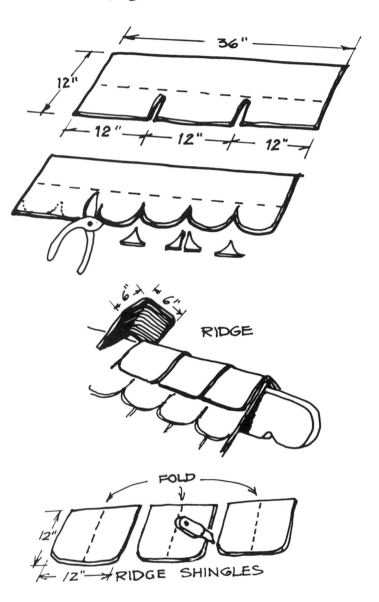

Step 4   **Finishing**

Add the windows and window trim (see Front Elevation on page 116).

Shed Playhouse

This practical backyard structure serves both kids and adults. The first floor is a 10 x 12-foot shed for storing bikes, tools, and garden equipment, while the top floor is a playhouse with a wrap-around deck. The shed features two doors that open 5 feet wide to accept large lawn mowing equipment, and two side windows to allow light in. The back wall is reserved for hanging tools.

The playhouse is accessed by a stairway *(see "Buildings Stairs" page 65)* in the back and has a walk-around deck on three sides. The Dutch door has a pointed-arched window, accented by two smaller windows in the front. The sides have the same size windows as the shed below giving the entire structure a sense of unity *(see Resources for windows on page 144).*

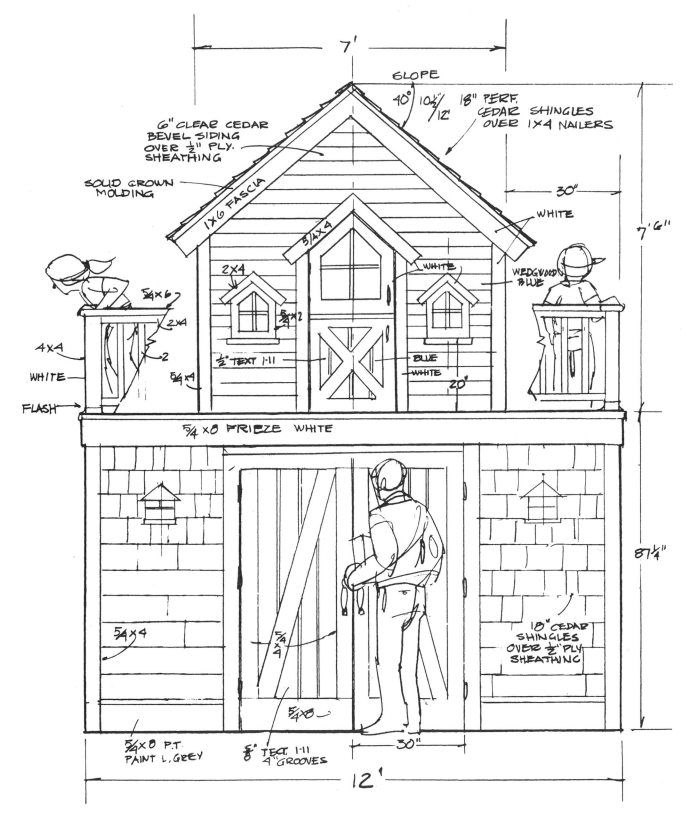

SLOPE

7'

40° 10½"/12"

6" CLEAR CEDAR BEVEL SIDING OVER ½" PLY. SHEATHING

18" PERF. CEDAR SHINGLES OVER 1X4 NAILERS

SOLID CROWN MOLDING

1X6 FASCIA

30"

5/4 X 4

WHITE

7'6"

WHITE

WEDGWOOD BLUE

2X4

5/4 X 6

2X4

5/4 X 2

4X4

2

WHITE

5/4 X 4

½" TEX1 1·11

BLUE WHITE

20"

FLASH

5/4 X 8 FRIEZE WHITE

5/4 X 4

5/4 X 4

87¼"

5/4 X 8

18" CEDAR SHINGLES OVER ½" PLY SHEATHING

5/4 X 8 P.T. PAINT L. GREY

⅝" TEX1 1·11 4" GROOVES

30"

12'

Front Elevation

You can build the shed/playhouse on a concrete slab foundation, however, considering the cost and difficulty involved in pouring a concrete foundation, a simple, pressure-treated wood base, supported by concrete blocks, is sufficient. This will also allow you to move it with a forklift if the situation arises.

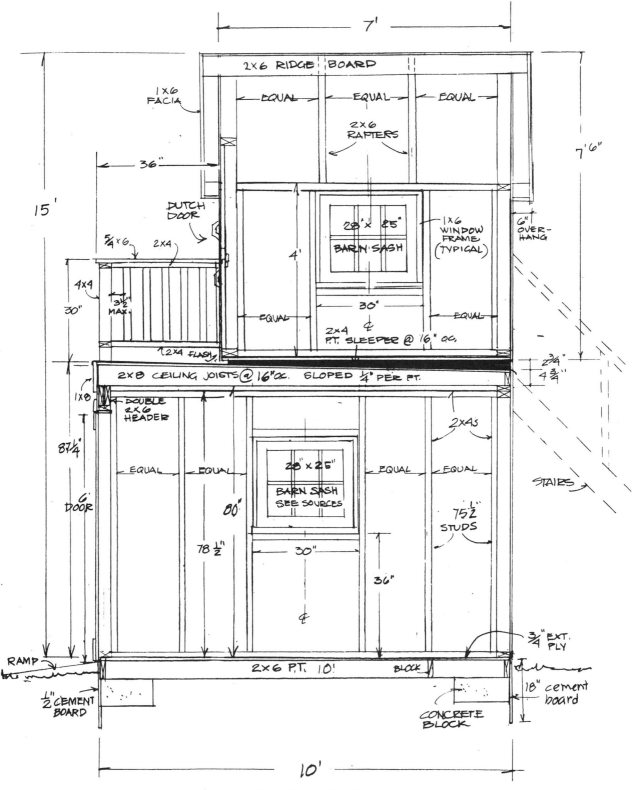

Side Cross Section

This project can be built in two stages. For instance, you could begin by building the shed in the fall, and continue in the spring with the playhouse addition on top. Build the shed with a flat roof, slightly pitched back, to drain off rainwater. Once the roof is completed, install 2x4 pressure-treated sleepers, on edge, 16 inches apart on-center. The space between spacers allows rainwater to run off. Then build the playhouse on top of the shed.

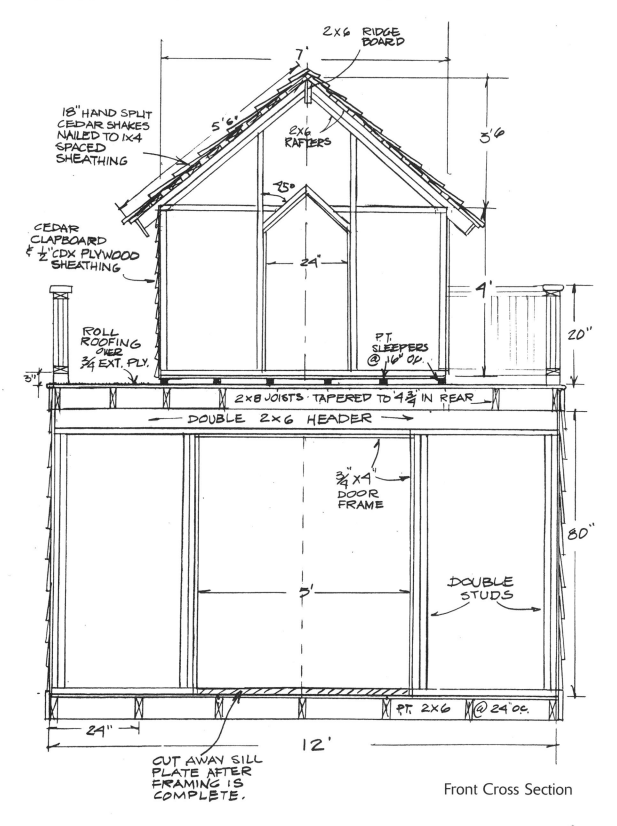

2x6 RIDGE BOARD

7'

5'6"

3'6"

18" HAND SPLIT CEDAR SHAKES NAILED TO 1x4 SPACED SHEATHING

2x6 RAFTERS

CEDAR CLAPBOARD & ½" CDX PLYWOOD SHEATHING

45°

24"

4'

ROLL ROOFING OVER ¾ EXT. PLY.

3"

P.T. SLEEPERS @ 16" O.C.

20"

2x8 JOISTS TAPERED TO 4¾" IN REAR

DOUBLE 2x6 HEADER

¾"x4" DOOR FRAME

5'

80"

DOUBLE STUDS

24"

12'

PT. 2x6 @ 24" O.C.

CUT AWAY SILL PLATE AFTER FRAMING IS COMPLETE.

Front Cross Section

✳ Materials List for Shed Unit

Quantity	Description	Length	Location
Base			
as needed	concrete blocks	8 x 8 x 16-inch	foundation
(6)	$1/2$-inch cement board	3x4 feet	foundation
(3)	2x6 P.T. lumber	12 feet	floor frame
(7)	2x6 P.T. lumber	10 feet	floor frame
(4)	$3/4$-inch P.T. ply.	4 x 8-foot sheets	floor frame
Walls			
(27)	2x4 #2 fir	8 feet	wall studs
(6)	2x4 #2 fir	10 feet	side plates
(5)	2x4 #2 fir	12 feet	front and rear plates
(2)	2x6 #2 fir	12 feet	double header
(10)	2x8 #2 fir	10 feet	ceiling joists
Roof			
(4)	$3/4$-inch P.T. ply.	4 x 8-foot sheets	roof
2 rolls	double coverage roll roofing		roof
as needed	roofing nails		roof
as needed	roofing cement		roof
Shed Walls			
(10)	$1/2$-inch CDX ply.	4 x 8-foot sheets	walls
(2)	$5/8$-inch texture #1–11 ply.	4 x 8-feet	doors
(6)	$5/4$ x4 #2 cedar	6 feet	door trim
(3)	1x6 #2 pine	6 feet	door frame
(4)	$5/4$x8 #2 cedar	12 feet	frieze and baseboard
(4)	$5/4$x8 #2 cedar	10 feet	frieze and baseboard
(5)	$5/4$x4 #2 cedar	14 feet	corner boards
Hardware			
(6)	$1^1/2$ x 3-inch strap hinges		door
(1)	thumb latch and lock		door
(2)	4-inch slide bolts		door
3 lbs.	6d galv. common nails		
2 lbs.	roofing nails		roof
5 lbs.	shingling nails		shingles
2 lbs.	6d box nails		
1 lb.	ring shank nails		
1 lb.	5d galv. finishing nails		
(1)	6 oz. Titebond III glue		
1 cartridge	PL 400 construction adhesive		

CDX ply. = APA-rated plywood sheathing; Exposure 1 (construction grade); galv. = galvanized; ply. = plywood; P.T. = pressure treated

Building the Shed

Step 1 **Constructing the Base Floor**

Choose a location that is well drained and easily accessible for both garden jobs and for kids to play. Stake out a 10 x 12-foot area and build a base floor frame using pressure-treated 2x6 lumber. Check to make sure it is square by placing a 4 x 8-foot sheet of plywood flush with two edges of the frame.

Place the floor frame on concrete blocks, resting on compacted earth. Make sure the floor frame is level on all sides and keep checking for level during construction, since the soil may compact further under weight. If this happens, jack the low end of the floor

frame up and insert slate shims between the concrete blocks and the wood floor frame.

To keep small animals from making a home under your shed, screw $1/2$-inch-thick cement board around the perimeter, cover the joints with fiberglass tape, and trowel a $1/8$-inch-thick layer of cement onto the cement board to give it a finished look. Nail sheets of $3/4$-inch exterior plywood to the top of the floor fame, using 6d flooring nails. Space the nails every 6 inches along the outside edges and 12 inches across the beams. Leave a $1/16$-inch space between panels to avoid buckling.

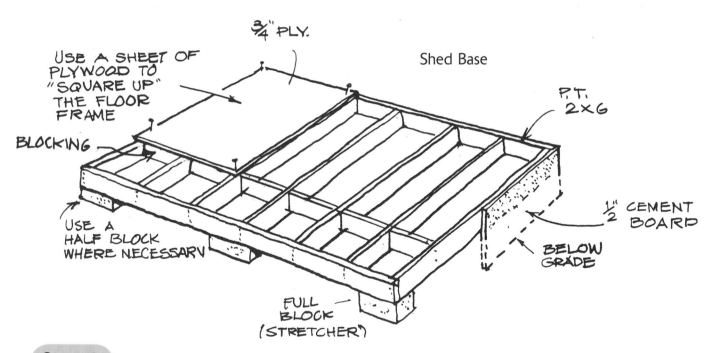

Shed Base

Step 2 **Framing the Walls**

Use the floor you just built as a giant worktable for building the wall frames. Tilt the walls up one at a time *(see page 130),* using temporary braces to hold them in place. Screw them together at the corners. The front wall supports a double 2x6 header that in turn supports nine 2x8 ceiling

joists *(see Front Cross Section on page 127).* To slope the roof, cut the ceiling joists so they taper towards the rear, pitching the roof at $1/2$-inch per foot. Cover the ceiling joists with a layer of $3/4$-inch plywood that also serves as the base for the playhouse *(see Side Cross Section on page 126).*

To waterproof the roof, apply a double layer of asphalt roll roofing, using roofing cement and roofing nails *(see Roll Roofing page 80)*.

Cover the walls of the shed with $1/2$-inch CDX plywood sheathing and trim the corners, windows, and doors with $5/4$ x 4 cedar boards. Trim the bottom walls with $5/4$x8 cedar boards, painted gray, to hide the unavoidable back splash from rain. Cover the plywood sheathing with 18-inch Perfection cedar shingles over tarpaper with a $7 1/2$-inch exposure.

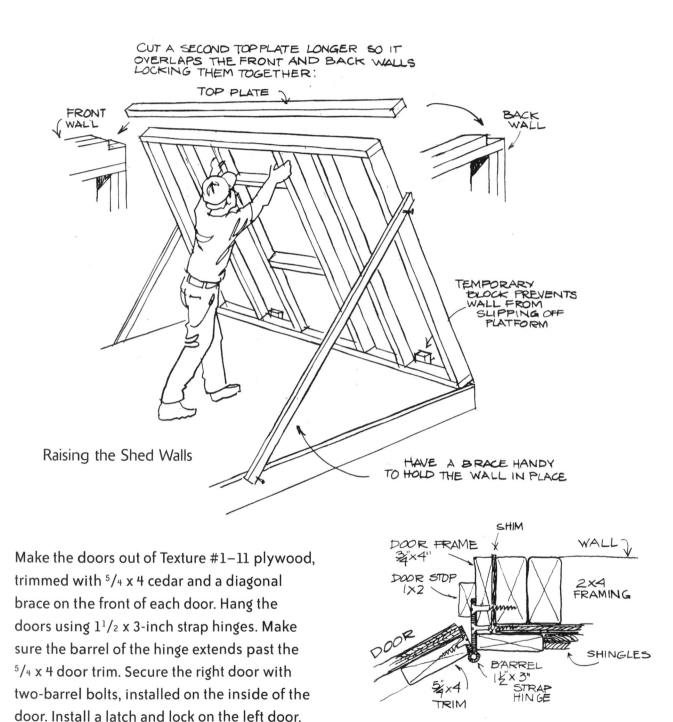

CUT A SECOND TOP PLATE LONGER SO IT OVERLAPS THE FRONT AND BACK WALLS LOCKING THEM TOGETHER:

TOP PLATE

FRONT WALL

BACK WALL

TEMPORARY BLOCK PREVENTS WALL FROM SLIPPING OFF PLATFORM

Raising the Shed Walls

HAVE A BRACE HANDY TO HOLD THE WALL IN PLACE

Make the doors out of Texture #1–11 plywood, trimmed with $5/4$ x 4 cedar and a diagonal brace on the front of each door. Hang the doors using $1 1/2$ x 3-inch strap hinges. Make sure the barrel of the hinge extends past the $5/4$ x 4 door trim. Secure the right door with two-barrel bolts, installed on the inside of the door. Install a latch and lock on the left door.

SHIM

DOOR FRAME $3/4$"x4"

WALL

DOOR STOP 1x2

2x4 FRAMING

DOOR

SHINGLES

$5/4$x4 TRIM

BARREL $1 1/2$" X 3" STRAP HINGE

Hinges

Quantity	Description	Length	Location
Base			
(6)	2x4 P.T. lumber	7 feet	sleepers
(2)	³/₄-inch P.T. ply.	4 x 8-foot sheets	sub-floor
(2)	³/₈-inch AC ply.	4 x 8-foot sheets	finished floor
(10)	2x4 studs	8 feet	walls
(4)	2x4 #2 fir	14 feet	plates
(6)	¹/₂-inch CDX ply.	4 x 8-foot sheets	walls
(2)	2x4 fir	12 feet	gables
(2)	2x6 fir	12 feet	rafters
Windows			
(4)	1x6 #2 pine	12 feet	window frames
(2)	28 x 25-inch barn sash windows *(see Resources)*		
(1)	¹/₈-inch Plexiglas	4 x 4-foot sheet	window
(1)	³/₄-inch MDO ply.	4 x 4-foot sheet	window
(1)	2x4 P.T. lumber	6 feet	windowsill
Door			
(1)	⁵/₈-inch texture #1–11	4 x 4-foot sheet	door
(2)	1x6 #2 pine	6 feet	door frame
(3)	⁵/₄x4 pine	8 feet	corner boards/door trim
275 lin. feet	6-inch clear cedar clapboard		
Roof			
(12)	1x4 #2 pine	14 feet	spaced sheathing for roof
(1)	2x6 #2 fir	8 feet	ridge board
(1)	36-inch-wide roll felt paper		roof
(2)	1x6 #2 pine	12 feet	front fascias
(1)	1x6 #2 pine	14 feet	side fascias
30 feet	solid crown molding		
6 bundles	hand-split shakes	24 inches	roof
Railings			
(1)	4x4 #2 cedar	12 feet	posts
(7)	2x4 clear cedar	12 feet	rails
(4)	⁵/₄x4 clear cedar	8 feet	handrails
128 lin. feet	2x2 #2 cedar		balustrades
Hardware			
(4)	1¹/₂ x 3-inch strap hinges		door
(2)	4-inch handles		door

AC ply. = A/C-grade exterior plywood; CDX ply. = APA-rated plywood sheathing Exposure 1 (construction grade); lin. feet = linear feet; total feet needed at random lengths; MDO ply. = medium density overlay plywood; P.T. = pressure treated

Building the Playhouse

Step 1

Support the playhouse with 2x4 pressure-treated sleepers, tapered at the same angle as the shed ceiling joists. This will make the playhouse floor level. Coat the sleepers with roofing cement and position them on top of the shed roof. Place a layer of ³/₄-inch pressure-treated plywood on top of the

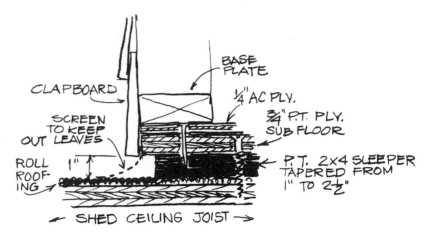

sleepers and screw it down, through the sleepers and into the roof below. Install a layer of ¹/₂-inch AC plywood over the ³/₄-inch plywood to improve the appearance of the floor on the inside of the playhouse. Frame the playhouse with 2x4s, 2x6 roof rafters, and ¹/₂-inch CDX plywood sheathing.

Step 2

To add interest to the playhouse walls, cover them with clear cedar clapboard (bevel siding), overlapping each course by 1 inch and staggering the joints. Butt the ends of the clapboards into ⁵/₄x4 corner boards.

Siding Detail

Step 3

Make the roof out of 1x4 spaced sheathing boards covered with 18-inch hand-split shakes. Frame the doors and windows with ⁵/₄x4 cedar boards.

Step 4

Make the door window by cutting a hole through the ¹/₂-inch Texture #1–11 sheathing, framing it on the inside and outside with ⁵/₄x4 cedar trim. Cut the two small flanking windows out of ³/₄-inch MDO plywood and fit and hinge them to the interior trim. For each window, cut and fit a ¹/₈-inch thick piece of Plexiglas and screw it to the back of the plywood.

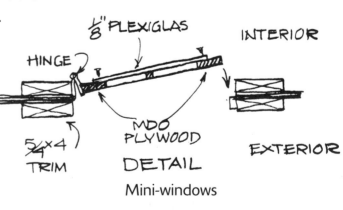

Mini-windows

Tip:

Drill extra large holes in the Plexiglas for the screws, allowing for expansion. Cut the sills for the windows (which open in) out of pressure-treated 2x4 lumber.

ACCESSORIES

Ladder Hoist

To protect yourself from "enemies" (ferocious dogs, skunks, and older brothers), hoist your ladder up into your treehouse, using a rope and pulley.

Making a Ladder Hoist

Tie a "bridle" rope around the top rung of the ladder. Tie another rope to the center of the bridle and run it up through a pulley somewhere high in the tree. On the other end of the rope, tie a bag of sand equaling the weight of the ladder. This will make it easier to haul the ladder up and also make it safer for anyone below when the ladder is lowered.

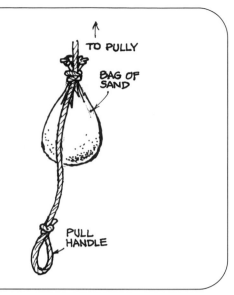

TO PULLY

BAG OF SAND

PULL HANDLE

Tips for Making Swings

- Swings can be made in less than a morning and last into adulthood. To make a swing, you need a piece of $3/4$-inch-diameter Dacron rope that measures twice the distance from the ground to the branch, plus an additional 6 feet. Don't use polypropylene (yellow) rope, as it can deteriorate in the sun—or nylon rope that has a tendency to stretch.

- To hang the swing, you need a ladder tall enough to reach the branch. For high branches you may need to rent or borrow an extension ladder, or hire a tree expert to climb the tree.

- Sand all the edges until they are smooth and free of splinters.

- Choose a branch that is relatively horizontal, about 10 to 12 feet from the ground. The lower the branch, the shorter the arc and the easier it will be for the rider to get up in the air.

On the following page is a simple method of putting up a fun swing. It can also be easily removed if you want to take it down later.

CAUTION:

Although swings may look harmless, they can end up causing accidents if caution is not taken. Children should be instructed not to walk or run in the path of a moving swing. It is impossible for the person swinging to stop. Many playgrounds have fenced-in swing areas for this reason.

Making a Simple Swing

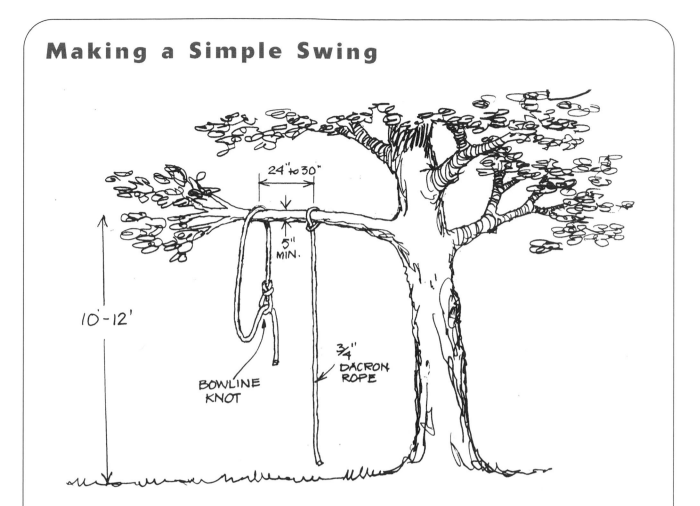

Step 1

Cut the rope into two pieces. Tie one end of each piece of rope around the branch, using a bowline knot *(see page 56)*. A bowline knot works well because it will not restrict the growth of the tree branch. It is also easier to untie, if necessary, and is one of the safest knots you can use. The two knots should ideally be 24 to 30 inches apart to give the swing a little more stability. If you want to protect the tree further, you can place a short length of rubber hose or carpet under the rope where it rubs against the tree branch.

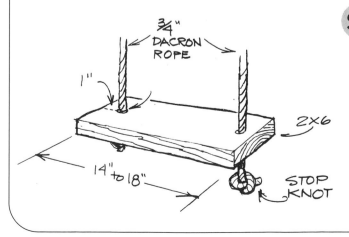

Step 2

Place the other end of each rope through one of the two holes in the seat and tie stop knots underneath. For the swing seat, you need a piece of 2x6 lumber, 14 to 18 inches long. Drill a $7/8$-inch-diameter hole, 1 inch in from each end of the board. Adjust the seat so that it is level. Test the swing and adjust the height, if necessary, by changing the knots under the seat.

Zip Line

For older kids who have treehouses, there is no quicker or more thrilling way to descend to the ground from a tree than riding a cabled trolley, also called a "zip line." Anyone using a zip line should follow some basic safety rules:

1. No pushing, shoving or horsing around while on the launching platform.

2. Each person should test the zip line while on the ground before using it.

3. Grip the handles firmly and don't let go until you reach the ground.

4. Make sure no one is in the way before launching and let everyone know that you are taking off by yelling "CLEAR!" "WATCH OUT!" or "HERE I COME!"

Before using the zip line for the first time, experiment with a bag of sand or dirt hung from the trolley by a rope. Adjust the height of the landing point and or the tightness of the cable so that the rider will come to a stop at the end of the ride and drop a few inches to the ground.

MARINE SHEVES (SEE SOURCES)

1½" DIA. HANDLE

¾" PLY.

TWO ALTERNATE HOMEMADE TROLLIES

METAL MARINE BLOCK

DETAIL

CRIMPED END

1" DIA. ALUM. TUBE

BICYCLE HANDLE

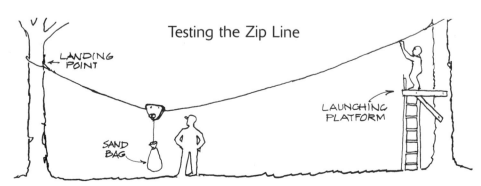

Testing the Zip Line

LANDING POINT

SAND BAG

LAUNCHING PLATFORM

TIP:

If building you own trolley seems like too much trouble, you can order the entire unit from a supplier (*see Resources on page 144*).

Message Board and Mirror

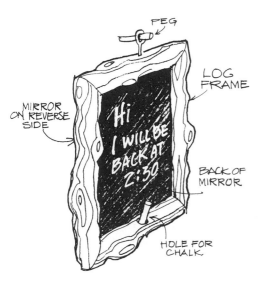

You may want to leave messages for your friends when you are away from your treehouse. This message board (about the size of this book) is easy to make from branches found in the woods. Cedar is the best wood to use but you can substitute other types of wood if cedar isn't available. Make sure to remove the bark and sand wood smooth. The message box can also serve as a mirror. Turn it around into the "mirror" position to keep your messages secret!

To safely cut the groove (dado) for the mirror, make a jig to hold the branch while it is being cut. Use a table saw for this (adults only). Place the branch inside the jig and drive several screws through the jig into the branch to hold it in place. Be careful not to screw the screws in too far so that they get in the path of the saw blade. When you finish the dado, cut the ends of the branches at a 45-degree angle and glue the mirror and frame.

Trash Box

Now and then your treehouse may get dirty and need to be swept out. Build a trap door in the floor in which to sweep leaves, acorns, candy wrappers. To catch trash, install a box underneath the floor that can be easily accessed, removed and emptied into a nearby trash can.

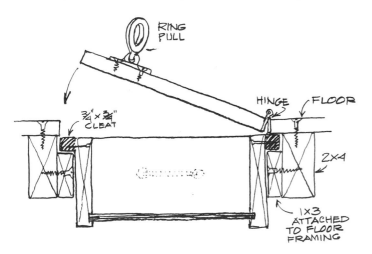

Bridges

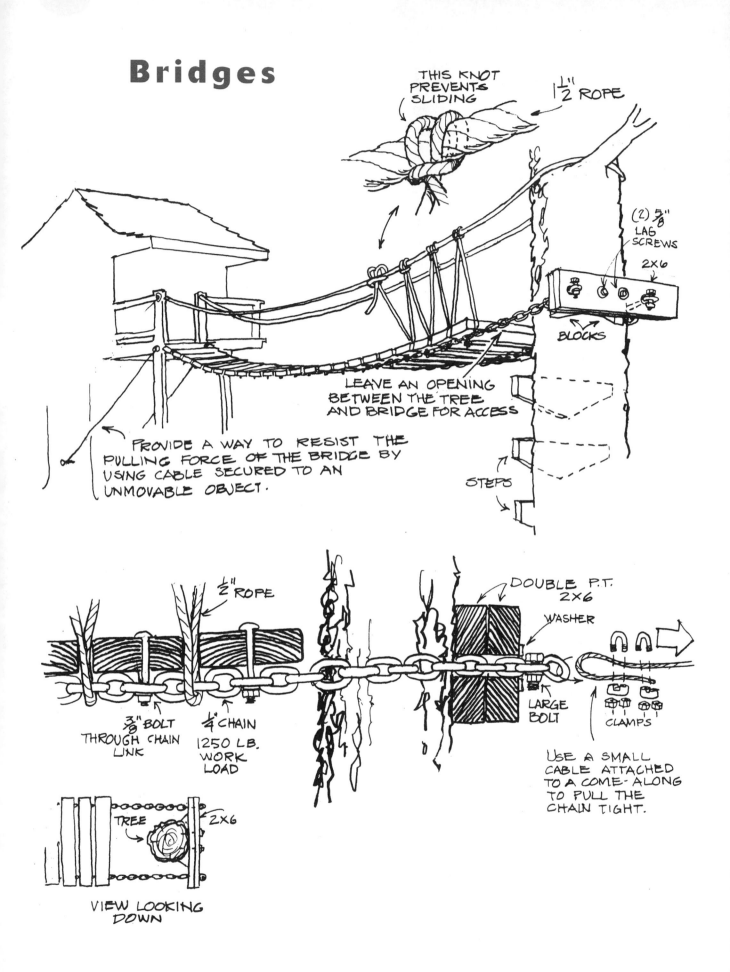

THIS KNOT PREVENTS SLIDING

1½" ROPE

(2) ⅝" LAG SCREWS

2×6

BLOCKS

LEAVE AN OPENING BETWEEN THE TREE AND BRIDGE FOR ACCESS

PROVIDE A WAY TO RESIST THE PULLING FORCE OF THE BRIDGE BY USING CABLE SECURED TO AN UNMOVABLE OBJECT.

STEPS

1½" ROPE

DOUBLE P.T. 2×6

WASHER

⅜" BOLT THROUGH CHAIN LINK

¼" CHAIN 1250 LB. WORK LOAD

LARGE BOLT

CLAMPS

USE A SMALL CABLE ATTACHED TO A COME-ALONG TO PULL THE CHAIN TIGHT.

TREE

2×6

VIEW LOOKING DOWN

Pulley and Basket

A pulley system can be quite helpful for lifting tools and materials into the tree while building your treehouse. Once the treehouse is built, you can use the pulley to haul up food, drinks, and other supplies.

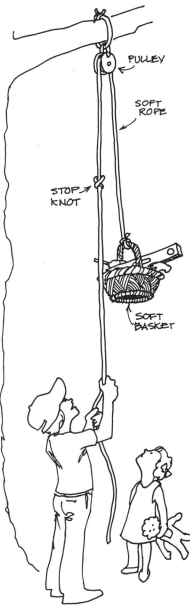

CAUTION:

In the excitement of hauling things up into the tree, the rope can slip out of your hands, sending the bucket down at a fast rate of speed and possibly hitting someone on the head. To prevent this from happening, tie a stop knot in the rope so that the basket will stop before it falls all the way down. As an added precaution, choose a basket that is made out of a soft material, like wicker, straw, or plastic.

Drawbridge

This easy-to-build drawbridge also serves as a door! Use a ³/₄-inch-thick piece of plywood, backed by two 1x4s to stiffen it. Hinge one end of the plywood to the doorsill and attach two ¹/₂-inch ropes to the other end. Run the ropes through two pulleys attached to the top of the doorframe. Connect the two ropes to a single rope used to pull the door (drawbridge) up.

Hoist

This ratchet-wheel hoist can lift things from the ground to the top of the treehouse. The flexible pawl makes a great sound and also acts as a safety feature preventing the bucket from falling down too quickly.

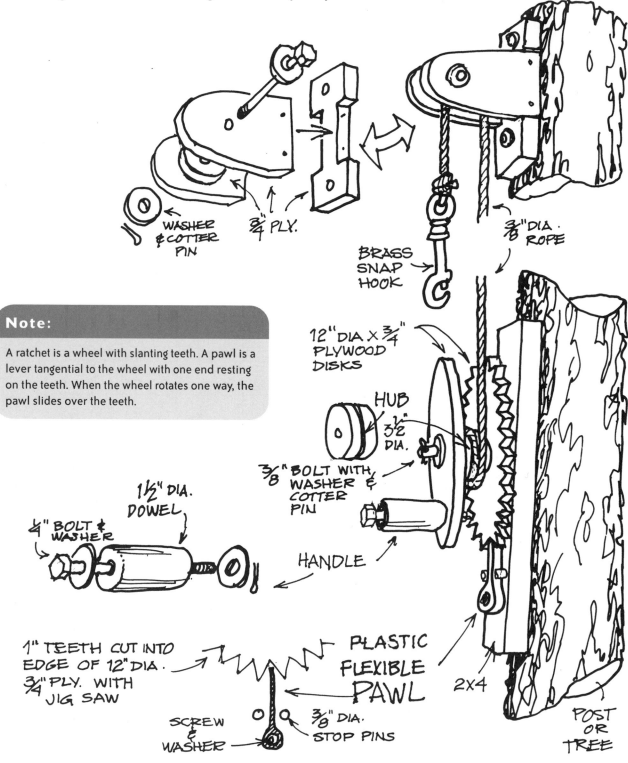

Note:

A ratchet is a wheel with slanting teeth. A pawl is a lever tangential to the wheel with one end resting on the teeth. When the wheel rotates one way, the pawl slides over the teeth.

WASHER & COTTER PIN

¾" PLY.

BRASS SNAP HOOK

⅜" DIA. ROPE

12" DIA x ¾" PLYWOOD DISKS

HUB

1½" DIA.

⅜" BOLT WITH WASHER & COTTER PIN

1½" DIA. DOWEL

¼" BOLT & WASHER

HANDLE

1" TEETH CUT INTO EDGE OF 12" DIA. ¾" PLY. WITH JIG SAW

PLASTIC FLEXIBLE PAWL

2x4

SCREW & WASHER

⅜" DIA. STOP PINS

POST OR TREE

Crow's Nest

This crow's nest (look-out point) is made from a half-barrel supported by a rack made out of scrap 2x4s. Begin by hoisting the barrel up into the tree using a rope and pulley tied to a branch that is located higher up in the tree. Once the barrel is hanging in place, build a rack, as shown in the illustration.

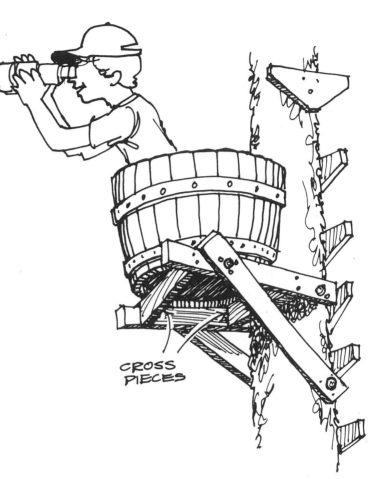

CROSS PIECES

Step 1

Construct and attach the two brace assemblies under the barrel and to the tree using $^3/_8$-inch lag screws. Join the two brace assemblies with two 2x4 crosspieces so they support the bottom of the barrel. Drill screws through the bottom of the barrel into the 2x4 brace assemblies and crosspieces. Once the brace assembly is in place, reinforce with additional 3-inch long screws.

Step 2

As an extra precaution, screw a $^1/_2$-inch lag screw through the wall of the barrel and into the tree.

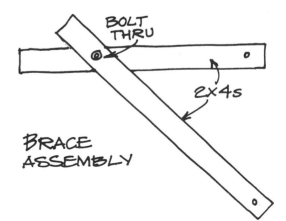

BOLT THRU

2X4s

BRACE ASSEMBLY

Pirate Ship Accessories

Pirate's Cutlass

You can make your own pirate cutlass out of a cardboard tube such as an old mailing tube or gift-wrapping tube. Cut the tube 22 inches long. Cut out a 5 x 13-inch hand guard from a piece of cardboard.

Step 1

Place the cardboard tube on the floor and step on it until it's completely flat. Cut out the shape of the hand guard from a piece of cardboard. Hold the end of the flattened tube on top of the cardboard, 1-inch from the end and trace the profile of the tube end with a pencil. Do the same at the other end.

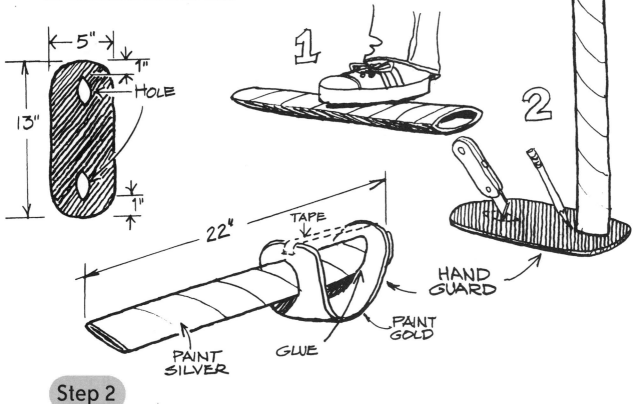

Step 2

Cut the two holes out using a utility knife. Bend the cardboard together and insert the end of the tube through the two holes. Glue the blade to the hand guard with white glue. Hold the two ends in place with a piece of tape while the glue is drying. Allow the glue to dry for two hours and then paint the blade silver and the hand guard gold.

Jolly Roger

To make this pirate flag, sketch in pencil two skull and cross-bones onto an old bed sheet, following the design shown here. Paint the background a flat black. This will help stiffen the cloth when it dries. Fold the flag over so the Jolly Roger shows on both sides and sew it onto the top of the backstay.

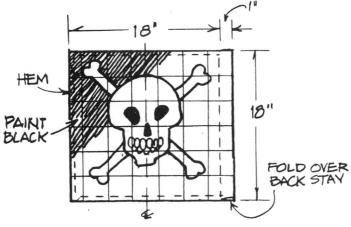

Ship's Wheel

This wheel can be made from a ³/₄-inch-thick piece of plywood, marked and cut to the dimensions shown in the illustration. Round off all sharp edges with sandpaper or a router. Mount the wheel to the stern mast with a ¹/₂ x 2-inch lag screw and washers.

THE PIE-RAT SHIPS STEERING WHEEL CAN BE MARKED AND CUT FROM A PIECE OF ¾" PLYWOOD AS SHOWN HERE

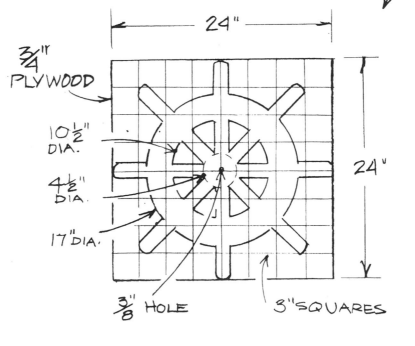

Resources

Antique Hardware

Van Dyke's Restorers
P.O. Box 278
Wonsocket, SD 57385
800-558-1234
www.vandykes.com

Auto Body Cement

Bondo (with 2.75 oz. hardener)
(available at auto supply and
hardware stores)

Bondo Corporation
3700 Atlanta Industrial
Parkway, NW
Atlanta, GA 30331
800-622-8754
www.bondo-online.com

Construction Adhesives

PL Premium Polyurethane
(available at hardware and
building supply stores)

OSI Sealants, Inc.
800-999-8920
www.stickwithpl.com

Liquid Nails (LN 950)
(available at hardware and
building supply stores)

Macco Adhesive
15885 West Sprague Road
Strongsville, OH 44136
800-634-0015
www.liquidnails.com

Gazebo Kits

(made to your specifications)

JR Woodcraft
15527 Hillside Road
St. Ignatius, MT 59865
406-745-2110

Hand Tools

(cable cutters, socket wrenches,
jacks, come-alongs, inner tubes)

Harbor Freight Tools
3491 Mission Oaks Boulevard
Camarillo, CA 93011
800-423-2567
www.harborfreight.com

Hardware

(and everything else)

McMaster-Carr Supply Co.
9630 Norwalk Boulevard
Santa Fe Springs, CA 90670
330-342-6100
www.mcmaster.com

Landscape Supplies

(cable, tree grips, stakes)

A.M. Leonard
241 Fox Drive
Piqua, OH 45356
800-543-8955
www.amleo.com

Lumber & Hardware

Lowe's Company Inc.
1605 Curtis Bridge Road
North Wilksboro, NC 28697
800-445-8641
www.lowes.com

Marine Hardware

(shackles, wire tope, chains)

Defender Industries, Inc.
42 Great Neck Road
Waterford, CT 06385
800-628-8225
www.defender.com

Power Tools

(cordless drills, miter saws)

Hitachi Koki USA, Ltd.
Atlanta, GA
800-206-7337
www.hitachi-koki.com

Pressure-Treated Wood (ACQ)

Chemical Specialties Inc.
200 East Woodland Road
Charlotte, NC 28217
800-421-8661
www.treatedwood.com

Pressure-Treated Wood Stain/Sealer

Osmose Wood Preserving, Inc.
980 Ellicott Street
Buffalo, NY 14209
716-882-5905
www.osmose.com

Rope

R&W Rope Warehouse
866-577-5505
39 Tarkiln Place
New Bedford, MA 02745
www.rwrope.com

Screws

SPAX Screws
6930 San Tomas Road
Suite 4
Elkridge, MD 21075
888-222-7729
www.spax.com

Synthetic Outdoor Ground Covers

SYNLawn
3060 Mercy Drive
Orlando, FL 32808
866-796-5296
www.synlawn.com

Tree Maintenance

(ropes, saws, etc.)

Bailey's
44650 Highway 101
Laytonville, CA 95454
800-322-4539
www.baileys-online.com

Thatched Roof Coverings

Bamboo Fencer
190 Concord Avenue
Cambridge, MA 02138
www.bamboofencer.com

Windows

Barn Sash Windows
(standard and custom sizes, made
from recycled plastic milk bottles)

Recycled Products
18294 Amber Road
Monticello, IA 52310
800-765-1489
www.recycledproductsco.com

Zip Lines

Spring Swings
2000 Avenue P
Suite 13
Riviera Beach, FL 33404
561-845-6966
www.springswings.com